Clarity in Chaos

With its fresh and deeply personal perspective on what it takes to lead with resilience and authenticity, this book challenges the traditional playbook on leadership by placing purpose at the core of every decision and action.

In a world increasingly defined by uncertainty and rapid change, leadership grounded in purpose is the compass that transforms uncertainty into impact, stagnation into growth, and vision into a legacy. Drawing on her extraordinary journey from technical safety expert to global executive, Megan Tranter weaves together compelling personal anecdotes, cutting-edge research, and practical tools to show how leaders can redefine success. But this book goes beyond strategies to invite readers into an authentic dialogue about vulnerability, growth, and the kind of leadership that transforms lives – not just spreadsheets. Readers will be left feeling understood, inspired, and empowered to take courageous actions in their careers, solving the pervasive problems of burnout, disconnection, and lack of fulfillment.

This book is the roadmap for seasoned executives and aspiring leaders to unlock their potential and lead with clarity and conviction.

Megan Tranter is a globally recognized leader, speaker, and career strategist who helps purpose-driven professionals elevate their leadership and achieve transformative impact. With over 20 years of experience at companies like Netflix, Amazon, and PepsiCo, Megan has held global executive roles in safety, ESG, and technology and is an avid advocate for creating values-driven workplaces that thrive in disruption.

Clarity in Chaos

Lead with Purpose in Disruptive Times

Megan Tranter

Routledge
Taylor & Francis Group
NEW YORK AND LONDON

Designed cover image: Getty Images

First published 2026
by Routledge
605 Third Avenue, New York, NY 10158

and by Routledge
4 Park Square, Milton Park, Abingdon, Oxon, OX14 4RN

Routledge is an imprint of the Taylor & Francis Group, an informa business

ISBN: 9781041041948 (hbk)
ISBN: 9781041033868 (pbk)
ISBN: 9781003627265 (ebk)

DOI: 10.4324/9781003627265

Typeset in Sabon
by codeMantra

To those who stand at the intersection of courage and compassion, who see beyond barriers and imagine workplaces that uplift and empower.

May you continue to drive change, lead with clarity, and inspire others to rise with purpose and resilience.

For all the risk-takers, innovators, and advocates for a brighter future – you are the legacy makers.

Contents

Introduction

Leadership Starts with Purpose

It's been 25 years since I wrote my first book. A technical tome written when I was an academic, teaching undergraduate and master's students in Australia and Hong Kong.

I was so proud of that book, putting my heart and soul into proving I could play with the big boys. I was determined to show that I had what it took to stand out, to make my mark, and to deliver something impactful and unforgettable.

I remember being politely informed by professional veterans that I was too young. Too inexperienced. And what could I possibly hope to contribute anyway?

But I had ambition.

I had dreams.

I was 26 years old.

I probably had no place writing a 407-page book.

To be fair, I didn't do it alone. I received a grant from the Australian Occupational Health and Safety Trust to partially fund the work. My parents-in-law secured a loan so that I could finance printing the run of 2,000 books. My friend designed the cover and illustrations. My sister proofread the manuscript. My dad and husband modeled for the photographs. My mom became the fulfillment center, as I filled her spare bedrooms with hundreds of boxes of heavy books and hooked up a fax machine to receive orders.

Why am I telling you this?

Because I had forgotten that all of these people didn't just support me, they shared my ambition. They saw my drive, my desire to prove myself, and they backed me. This is a theme that has followed me throughout my career.

That you don't walk through your career alone.

And that ambition isn't enough.

Success – real, lasting success – requires clarity and resilience. Adapting even when faced with disruption or uncertainty. It's about navigating with

DOI: 10.4324/9781003627265-1

a steady focus, being willing to pivot, and understanding that leadership isn't about what you achieve but how you lift up others.

Fast forward five years after publishing that book, and I don't think I would have ever imagined that I would have found myself halfway around the world.

Sitting on an international flight, 36 weeks pregnant, and about to start a new life. Leaving my career in Australia behind and, at the same time, fulfilling my biggest dream of moving to the United States. *Was I crazy? What did the world hold for me?*

I cried for what felt like the entire flight. I remember the kind flight attendant asking, "Did you leave someone behind?" As I wiped my tears away, I didn't know how to answer. Yes, I was leaving behind one life. But I was also starting a new life. A life that would ultimately bring my career to giddy heights. A global executive at some of the world's biggest companies and well-known brands.

A career that would lead me to the United Nations in NYC, launching a multi-company initiative to improve road safety; to Washington DC, where I'd meet with politicians and their staff in the halls of power; to leading global teams in the thousands; and to working alongside some of the most inspiring colleagues imaginable.

All while doing work that made my soul sing. Leading purpose-driven work.

Because without purpose, leadership can feel hollow. Like you're going through the motions without a clear destination. But when you have a purpose, it brings clarity, energy, and direction. Not only to leaders but also to everyone around them.

So, what exactly is purpose-driven work?

At its core, it's the pursuit of something greater than personal achievement. It's about creating impact, driving positive change, and knowing that what you do each day has meaning beyond the metrics.

Not that goals and metrics aren't important. Goal setting and measuring success (and failure) *are* important. But perhaps the message is that at some point, we realize that success in and of itself, may not be the worthy outcome. And that today's measure of success, as defined by others, may not be *your* measure of success.

After all, purpose-driven work isn't just about setting goals. It's about aligning those goals with values that resonate deeply within you and the people you lead. It's work that fuels you, that sustains you through challenges, and that connects you to something larger than yourself.

As I moved through the highs and lows of my career, I saw that purpose-driven leadership wasn't a one-time decision. It was something that required constant nurturing and, sometimes, recalibration. Purpose evolves as we grow, as our experience shapes us, and as we learn what truly matters.

Leading with purpose means having the courage to stay aligned with your values even when faced with hard decisions, when the path isn't clear, or when disruption shakes the ground beneath you. As John C. Maxwell[1] wisely put it,

> A leader is one who knows the way, goes the way, and shows the way.

But what happens on the days you don't know the way? Or when the path ahead seems hazy at best?

The truth is that every leader, whether they are a seasoned executive or just starting out, has days like this. One day, you feel unstoppable. Next, something seems missing.

That feeling of being stuck isn't a failure. It's a sign. A signal that something deeper is calling you to elevate your leadership.

This book is about answering that call and moving from feeling stuck to soaring as a purpose-driven leader, one who shapes their career and leaves a meaningful impact on the world around them.

Why This Book, Why Now?

Unlike my first book, this one is not an academic text. Don't worry. You won't find a periodic table anywhere. I've tried to make it a comprehensive, practical guide to address various issues affecting purpose-driven professionals. Topics like feeling stuck, understanding your unique value proposition, making courageous decisions to build a brilliant career, and having resilience.

Based on the feedback and encouragement of colleagues and clients, I finally decided that at some point, I should bring the ideas and experiences from my career and consulting practice in one place. That time is now.

Over the years, I learned that when leaders start with purpose, they inspire a sense of belonging and commitment in others. They are able to build resilience in their teams, not just by setting strategic goals, but by grounding those goals into something meaningful.

We're living in times of unprecedented complexity. The pace of change is relentless. I'm sure you're seeing it and feeling it. Technological leaps, social shifts, global crises. The world is moving so fast, and it sometimes feels impossible to keep up.

And shall we even talk about the old models of leadership that thrived on control, hierarchy, and short-term gains? They're crumbling. Fast.

Today, leaders need to be agile, resilient, and, most importantly, purpose-driven.

Purpose-driven leaders don't just seek personal success. They want to make a difference, to leave things better than they found them. They know their work contributes to something bigger, whether creating a healthier workplace, advancing social change, or building products that positively impact lives.

Purpose-driven leaders are people like Mary Barra[2] at General Motors, who has emphasized inclusivity and a vision for a future with zero crashes, zero emissions, and zero congestion. Or someone I had first-hand experience working with, Indra Nooyi,[3] the former Chairman and CEO at PepsiCo, who was the original architect of *Performance with Purpose*.

I joined PepsiCo in 2007, just after the *Performance with Purpose* initiative was formally introduced in 2006. At the time, it was a bold step, and as an employee, I felt incredibly proud working for a company committed to social responsibility and sustainability while delivering business success. It was a *triple bottom line* in action. And now, almost two decades later, it has stood the test of time even as it has been succeeded by PepsiCo Positive (pep+), which strives to create a more sustainable and resilient food system for the future, under the new CEO Ramon Laguarta.

My Journey with Purpose-Driven Leadership

As a graduate in the 1990s, I was one of Australia's first university students in health and safety. I remember my first week, when everything I knew about physics was covered in a three-hour lecture. Struggling with chemistry concepts, not to mention studying for what felt like a hundred hours for a statistics exam. You see, I was completing the same courses as future optometrists, podiatrists, and environmental health officers.

In my final year, I asked my professor:

"What job will I get, and what will I be called?"

The answer was disappointing and, honestly, confusing.

"You're an occupational health and safety professional."

"Excuse me? That's not a real job."

Despite this confusion, I entered the big, wide world of work, thinking my superpower was my technical expertise. So long as I knew how to interpret the regulations. Or write a policy document. Or complete an audit.

That's how I measured my impact.

After all, that's what university had taught me.

But that wasn't it. That wasn't purposeful work.

It all changed for me on a hot summer day. I was in my office on beautiful Sydney Harbour when the phone rang. An employee at the company I worked for had flipped their car in a rural area, suffering critical injuries. I didn't know them. But for a split second, I imagined their face. A person like me, someone with a family, dreams, and plans for the future.

In that instant, the world became sharper and colder. The distance between me and the people affected by others' decisions collapsed into that single, heart-stopping moment on the phone. I couldn't stop picturing them. I imagined their family receiving the call, the rush to the hospital, and the dread that must have filled the air. It struck me that, until then, I had thought of my career as a job.

Build a strategy.

Compile actions.

Complete the tasks.

Rinse and repeat.

But now, the weight of responsibility felt real and profound, like a promise I had unknowingly broken. Those experiences taught me something deeply transformative about purpose-driven leadership.

It isn't about possessing all the answers. Instead, it's about having the courage to ask the right questions, to dig deeper, and to stay grounded in a set of values that can withstand any storm.

Leadership, I realized, isn't about certainty. It's about holding steady in uncertainty and finding the strength to stay curious and open, especially when the answers feel just out of reach.

When the pressures of change loomed and the stakes felt impossibly high, purpose became my North Star.

It was the quiet, unwavering guide that reminded me why I was here and what I was meant to do. Purpose helped me stay anchored in the darkest moments and urged me to create a meaningful impact even when I wasn't sure what lay ahead. It showed me that true resilience isn't about being unbreakable. It's about finding the will to rebuild, to adapt, and to keep moving forward.

With purpose as my foundation, I found the strength to show up, to advocate fiercely, and to build a culture where others could find their own sense of meaning.

This book isn't your typical guide to leadership tactics and tools (though you'll find plenty of actionable strategies here). It's about rethinking leadership from the inside out and aligning every decision and every action with the values that define who you are and what you stand for. It's about building the kind of resilience that doesn't just help you endure uncertainty but empowers you to rise within it to turn challenges into moments of growth and impact.

I wrote this book for leaders who crave something deeper from their careers than just results. If you're ready to lead with purpose, step into a new level of influence grounded in authenticity, and create a legacy that endures beyond quarterly reports, this book will be your guide through that transformation.

In these pages, you'll find not just strategies but a new perspective: one that calls you to lead from a place of conviction, embrace vulnerability as a strength, and harness the power of purpose as your compass. Together, we'll explore what it means to lead with a whole heart, cultivate resilience that empowers rather than hardens, and build a career that feels successful and meaningful.

Because leadership isn't about the titles or the accolades. It's about the impact you create, the values you live by, and the legacy you leave in the lives of others.

What's Inside: From Feeling Stuck to Soaring

My career has had days where I walked the dusty, long wall of an underground coal mine. Bumped along in the cab of a noisy truck while chatting with truck drivers who were making an honest living. Then, there were days when I boarded the company jet, flying halfway across the world, hopping from factory to factory. And there were the moments I sat in a boardroom, presenting to top executives with sweaty palms and a heartbeat that betrayed the stakes of the moment.

The journey through these chapters mirrors the path I took in my own leadership evolution, rooted in scientific and business research and the lessons learned from real-world experiences. When you start your career in a technical area like I did, it sometimes takes a little while to realize that there is more to work (and life) than the metrics, the treadmill of deadlines, and the daily push to "get things right."

It's easy to get caught up in the mechanics. The numbers. The reports. The perfectly followed procedures.

For me, the turning point was understanding that real success isn't just about the precision of your work. It's about the purpose behind it.

I began to see that the most meaningful parts of my job weren't the metrics themselves but the impact those metrics had on people's lives. I realized that a leader's role isn't just to deliver results, but to create a culture that makes those results matter.

As we move through these chapters, you'll find that leadership is less about maintaining control and more about embracing growth. It's about asking yourself: *How can I make a difference here? How can I move beyond the numbers to inspire real change?*

You'll learn to look beyond the surface-level achievements and to recognize that authentic leadership is found in the courage to evolve, the resilience to face challenges head-on, and the commitment to foster an environment where everyone can thrive.

We'll begin by anchoring ourselves in the concept of purpose. Why it's essential, how to define it, and how it becomes the driving force that keeps us aligned in moments of doubt.

Purpose isn't just a feel-good phrase. It's the bedrock of true impact.

Once we connect with our purpose, we'll confront the trap of stagnation and discover strategies to break free. We'll delve into what it means to lead boldly, build a leadership presence that resonates, and master the art of positive influence.

From there, we'll immerse ourselves in resilience. Learning how to cultivate it within ourselves, embed it in our teams, and weave it into the culture of our organizations. Resilience isn't about avoiding falls but discovering the inner strength to rise each time.

Then, we'll dive into the topic of creativity and innovation. Neuroscience reveals that environments rich in psychological safety and cognitive diversity encourage people to bring forth their best ideas. You'll gain strategies to create spaces where people don't just perform but they actually thrive, transforming daily work into avenues for growth and inspiration.

In the chapter dedicated to legacy-building, we'll examine how purpose-driven leaders create lasting impact by staying true to their core values and envisioning goals beyond short-term wins. Along the way, we'll explore the critical role of psychological safety, the transformative power of a growth mindset, and other research-backed approaches that boost performance, deepen engagement, and build a foundation for enduring success.

So, Let's Begin

As you read these pages, I invite you to look inward and reflect on your own leadership story.

Where do you feel the weight of being stuck?

What holds you back from soaring?

Who is the leader you aspire to become?

These questions are deeply personal and universally felt, and I hope this book will offer you the tools, insights, and inspiration to explore and answer them honestly and with courage.

Remember, leadership isn't about perfection. It's about growth, resilience, and, above all, purpose. It's about shaping your leadership to accurately reflect who you are and what you want to accomplish. Not only in this moment but also in the years that lie ahead.

As you embark on this journey, remember that you don't need all the answers, but you do need to be willing to ask the questions that matter most. You have within you the courage to step forward, the resilience to keep going, and the purpose to make a difference.

So take a breath, and take that first step. Let this be a path you walk and a story you create. One of impact, integrity, and a legacy that endures.

Together, let's turn the page and begin.

Notes

1 Maxwell, J. C. 2011. *The Leadership Handbook: 26 Critical Lessons Every Leader Needs*. Thomas Nelson.
2 Stanford Report. 2024. "Mary Barra on Leadership and Innovation." *Stanford News*, August 23. https://news.stanford.edu/stories/2024/08/mary-barra.
3 Nooyi, I. 2021. *My Life in Full: Work, Family, and Our Future*. Portfolio.

Chapter 1

The Quiet Call for More

"Megan, are you happy with where you are?"

That June day in 2015, the question caught me completely off guard. I was hosting a global team conference in Ireland. Sunlight filtered through the branches of old oak trees surrounding the country house where we were staying, casting a serene, almost magical glow over everything.

The team had been immersed in a week of strategic planning, balanced with moments of relaxation and renewal. Sound baths, mindfulness sessions, and quiet walks in the countryside. The days were filled with lively discussions and bold ideas yet threaded with a sense of calm and connection that only this setting could offer. It was a rare blend of focus and tranquility, where work met well-being and big-picture thinking felt as natural as the rolling hills outside our window.

On the surface, it looked like a scene from a dream that marked years of hard work, success, and a career others might envy. But as I sat there, hearing those words, I realized I had no answer.

Was I happy?

I looked around, my mind racing through the achievements, the milestones, and all the moments I thought would bring me fulfillment. And yet, beneath it all, there was a quiet emptiness.

A sense that, despite everything I'd built, something was missing.

It wasn't that I disliked the work. It was a deeper feeling, a realization that somewhere along the way, I had drifted from the purpose that once ignited my passion.

The question lingered, following me in the days and weeks that followed, pressing into my thoughts and challenging everything I thought I knew about success. I wondered if I'd been living on autopilot and moving forward without direction or meaning.

I realized that somewhere, somehow, I'd lost touch with the *why* that had always driven me.

And so, that one question became a catalyst. It made me confront some hard truths, dig deep, and ask myself:

DOI: 10.4324/9781003627265-2

Where was I really going?
Who did I want to become as a leader?
Was I ready to change and move toward a life aligned with my values?

That was the beginning of a journey. Not just to rediscover my purpose but to reimagine my career in a way that aligned with the things I valued most.

There comes a moment in every career when you might ask yourself, "Is this really all there is?"

You've achieved success, climbed the ladder, and maybe even garnered a few awards along the way. And yet, a quiet, persistent hum of dissatisfaction lingers. At first, it's barely noticeable. But over time, that hum grows louder until it becomes unmistakable: *you're not where you want to be.*

This feeling isn't about a lack of ambition or skill. It's a universal experience for professionals across all industries and career stages.

Psychologists call it *career stagnation*,[1] and it's the sense that you've plateaued, stuck in a routine that no longer excites or challenges you.

So how do you recognize when you've hit this crossroad?

And more importantly, how do you break free and move forward?

This chapter is about recognizing the signs that you're in a rut and transforming that discomfort into a powerful springboard for growth. Together, we'll explore the telltale signs of career stagnation, drawing from research, real-life examples, and some of my own experiences.

Recognizing When You're Stuck

> To improve is to change; to be perfect is to change often.
>
> – Winston Churchill

It's easy to brush off feelings of dissatisfaction as a temporary slump or blame them on external factors. I'm sure you've experienced them: a challenging project, a difficult manager, or the general grind of everyday work. But when that discontent lingers, it's worth paying attention.

I once spoke to a colleague who had been a rising star in her field. Emily was admired by her peers, sought after for high-stakes projects, and had achieved success by every traditional metric. Yet, she felt unfulfilled, haunted by a quiet sense that something was missing. She'd chalked it up to stress at first, to the demands of balancing her career with recently returning to work after the birth of her twins. But as time passed, she realized this feeling wasn't fleeting.

It was something deeper.

That realization that her discontent had roots beyond a "bad week" or a heavy workload was the first sign that she might be stuck. She'd reached a point where success alone no longer felt like enough.

If you've felt something similar, here are some signs that you, too, might be in a rut:

A Loss of Passion: The excitement that once fueled you has dulled, and you find yourself going through the motions rather than feeling genuinely engaged. What used to inspire you now feels like a chore.

And although pragmatists may tell us to not follow our passion with our career, you might know what it feels like to lose it. That's because passion drives engagement, creativity, and growth. It makes us feel good and fuels intrinsic motivation – the kind of motivation that encourages you to seek out challenges, innovate, and go beyond the bare minimum. So when you lose it, you lose more than just enthusiasm. You lose momentum. And work can feel like an endless cycle of tasks rather than an opportunity for growth.

Questioning Your Purpose: There's a quiet but persistent question in the back of your mind: *Is this really what I want?* You start wondering if your current path is aligned with your deeper values and long-term goals. The feeling of losing connection to your work's purpose can be unsettling. What once aligned with your values now feels distant, and the passion you once had has waned.

Purpose in life is associated with less subjective stress,[2] so it's perhaps not surprising that when your sense of purpose begins to fade, stress and dissatisfaction can creep in. Without a clear "why" driving your work, the challenges you face can feel heavier, and even minor setbacks can seem overwhelming.

This can manifest in subtle but powerful ways. You might notice a lack of motivation to tackle new projects, an increasing reluctance to voice ideas, or a tendency to avoid professional development opportunities. But questioning your purpose doesn't mean you're failing. This period of reflection can be an invitation to realign your work with your values and rediscover what truly matters.

When I was deeply embedded in purpose-driven leadership roles, I loved feeling connected to a bigger "why." They were existential "whys": climate change, human rights, and the well-being of communities. And these were more than just abstract ideals.

They were causes that fueled my commitment and guided me through long days and difficult decisions. I knew my work wasn't just about hitting targets. I felt like I was making a difference in the world by protecting the planet and improving lives in ways beyond what could be measured on a spreadsheet.

That sense of purpose was my anchor. A reminder that every small action contributed to something far larger than myself. A collective effort to build a future worth living in, not just for us but for generations to come.

But if you've lost sight of your purpose, if you're in a role that no longer resonates with your values, then it might be time to reassess.

Lack of Progress: According to Harvard researcher Dr. Teresa Amabile[3] and researcher Dr. Steven Kramer, the feeling of making progress in meaningful work can boost motivation and morale. This is known as the **Progress Principle.** And without this sense of forward movement, our drive and enthusiasm quickly diminish. If you haven't felt that rush of accomplishment lately, it might be a sign that your career is in a holding pattern.

Lack of Personal Growth: You've stopped learning or feel that you're no longer challenged. The days start blending together, and it seems like you're on a loop, doing the same tasks without any sense of growth or progression.

Persistent Restlessness: You can't shake the feeling that you're meant for something more. Even on good days, when you're productive, and things are running smoothly, there's an underlying itch for something different.

Emotional Detachment: You begin to feel distant from your work, colleagues, or the organization as a whole. You might catch yourself feeling indifferent about things that once mattered.

Physical and Mental Fatigue: Feeling exhausted by work that once energized you isn't the same as burnout from overwork. It's the slow drain that happens when tasks lack significance. The World Health Organization[4] defines burnout as a syndrome resulting from chronic workplace stress that has not been successfully managed, characterized by energy depletion, increased mental distance from one's job, and reduced professional efficacy. Sound familiar?

Fear of Change: Even if you recognize that you're stuck, the fear of making a change can keep you from taking action. Fear is a big topic and something we will talk about later in this book. It's something that can paralyze even the most ambitious and capable individuals. The fear of stepping into the unknown and leaving the familiar behind can feel overwhelming. *What if the change doesn't work out? What if you fail? What if you regret leaving the stability of your current role?* These "what if's" can create a mental fog, clouding your ability to see the potential opportunities that lie ahead.

I've changed roles and companies quite often. At the beginning of my career, I took a new job every two years or so. I've also stayed with companies for almost a decade. Believe me, every change didn't come without fear. *What do people think of me? Can't she hold down a job? Is there something wrong with her?*

Fear often stems from our brain's natural inclination to prioritize safety and certainty. It's wired to resist risk and cling to what it knows, even if staying put means remaining unhappy or unfulfilled. This protective mechanism, while well-intentioned, can keep you tethered to a situation that no longer serves you.

But here's the paradox: change is often the catalyst for *growth*. By confronting fear and taking that first step, you open the door to new possibilities, fresh perspectives, and the chance to reignite your passion and purpose.

Just remember, it's not about eliminating fear but learning to move forward despite it. Later in this book, we'll explore practical strategies to reframe fear, build courage, and take action, even when uncertainty feels daunting. For now, recognize that fear, while intimidating, is also a sign that you're on the edge of something transformative.

Finally, one of the clearest indicators of stagnation is **The Autopilot Effect**. Have you ever driven to work, arrived, and barely remembered the drive itself? That's autopilot, a habit loop that requires little conscious thought.

When this happens in your career, you're coasting. You're completing tasks without real engagement, simply going through the motions. This often happens when your work no longer challenges you. Yes, the job gets done, but without excitement or passion.

I remember a phase in my own career where I could compile global strategic plans, prepare reports, and present to stakeholders without breaking a mental sweat. And while that sounds efficient, it felt empty. I was doing my job, but I wasn't growing or stretching. Autopilot had taken over, and it was draining my sense of purpose.

Take a moment to reflect: how many of these signs resonate with you? If some of them hit close to home, you're likely experiencing career stagnation.

But don't worry. Recognizing it is the first step toward transforming it. This isn't about casting judgment on where you are but acknowledging that something needs to change. Transformation begins the moment we become aware and continues as we learn to face our discomfort and listen closely to what it's telling us.

So, if you identify with any of these feelings, take it as a signal. This could be the start of something profound, a chance not only to break free from what's holding you back but also to step into a version of yourself that feels genuinely fulfilled and aligned.

Activity 1 Reflect and Realign

Take some time to step back and examine your career. This exercise will help you identify areas where you might feel "stuck" and consider ways to realign with your values and goals.

1 **Spot the Signs:** On a sheet of paper, list each sign of career stagnation. Next to each, jot down if and how you experience it. Be candid. This is a moment for awareness, not judgment.
2 **Uncover the Source:** For each sign that resonates, ask yourself: *What's driving this feeling? If you feel restless, what are you craving? If you've lost passion, what no longer feels meaningful?* If you're questioning your purpose, envision a path that could feel fulfilling.
3 **Visualize Your Future:** Imagine yourself a year from now, feeling engaged and purposeful. *What does a day in that life look like?* Capture specific details about both your work and personal sense of fulfillment.
4 **Take One Small Step:** Review what you've written and choose one action you can take this week to address any feelings of stagnation. Maybe it's reaching out to a mentor, signing up for a new course, or dedicating time to explore inspiring career options. Commit to that one step as a move toward your more aligned future.

Remember, transformation unfolds gradually. Each small step builds momentum toward a career path that's both fulfilling and aligned with your purpose.

The Success Trap: When Achievement Holds You Back

Interestingly, career stagnation often strikes high achievers the hardest. This phenomenon, known as the **Success Trap**, is a paradox that surprises many ambitious professionals. Here's how it typically unfolds:

You master your role.

You become the go-to person for solving specific problems.

You receive recognition, rewards, or promotions.

Eventually, you find yourself boxed into doing more of the same.

In fact, you're so exceptional at what you do that stepping outside your niche feels almost impossible. I know this trap well. I had a reputation for delivering results in every project I took on, becoming the person who could get things done.

But over time, the very success that had built my reputation began to feel like a cage. I was called on for the same types of projects, solving the same problems, and while I was effective, I wasn't growing. My career, once filled with excitement and challenge, had become a routine I couldn't break.

I had to confront a hard truth. The path that had once propelled me forward was now holding me back. To move beyond this, I had to leap away from the familiar, away from what I knew I could do well, and step into new territory where I could rediscover that sense of growth and possibility.

Breaking out of the success trap isn't easy, but it's essential to keep evolving. It requires courage, curiosity, and a willingness to stretch beyond the comfort of past achievements.

Breaking Out of Stagnation

Stagnation is not a permanent state, but it is a signal for change. Here are some practical strategies to help you break free and regain momentum:

Reignite Your Curiosity: One of the simplest ways to shake up your routine is by learning something new. Learning novel skills can rewire the brain and enhance creativity, cognitive flexibility, and mood.[5] But don't worry, you don't have to sign up for formal courses. Exploring new projects, experimenting with a different area, or even diving into a side interest can do wonders.

Many companies value *curiosity* as a core value, and you can probably understand why. It drives innovation, fosters adaptability, and keeps teams and organizations competitive in a rapidly changing world. Curious employees ask the right questions, challenge the status quo, and bring fresh perspectives to the table. In fact, curiosity often becomes the secret ingredient for breakthroughs, whether it's finding a creative solution to a persistent problem or uncovering an opportunity that others overlooked.

Curiosity isn't just about being inquisitive. Being open to new experiences and ideas or looking at challenges as opportunities to grow rather than obstacles to avoid, is the secret sauce. And when nurtured, curiosity has a ripple effect. A curious mindset can inspire others around you, creating a culture of continuous learning and improvement.

Take my own experience, for example. There was a season in my career where I felt stuck in the day-to-day routine of my role. I was working at a tech company, often meeting with software teams yet not fully understanding how they worked or what they did. I was certainly curious but didn't think I'd have the time to learn how to code or change careers. *What did I do?*

I took a role leading a team of product and program managers, working on an enterprise-level software solution. I learned about software development and product roadmaps and embraced a completely new way of thinking. It wasn't always smooth. Believe me, there were moments of self-doubt and imposter syndrome. But each time I asked a question or dove into a concept I didn't understand, I felt that spark of discovery reignite.

Curiosity doesn't demand that you know everything. It simply demands that you care enough to explore and reminds us that it's okay to not have all the answers, as long as you're willing to search for them. And often, the most rewarding paths are the ones you hadn't planned for but chose to follow anyway.

> **Activity 2 Curiosity Challenge**
>
> Think of one area unrelated to your expertise that you're interested in exploring. Spend 30 minutes this week learning something about it. Read an article, listen to a podcast, or watch a tutorial. Write down what you learned and any insights you gained about how it connects (or could connect) to your current role.

Seek Out Feedback: Asking for honest feedback from peers, mentors, or supervisors can help you identify areas where you may have plateaued. Often, those around us can see our growth potential more clearly than we can.

They may notice areas where we could push further, where we could step up, or where we might benefit from a shift in focus. Feedback, though not always easy to hear, is often what we need to step out of our comfort zone and stretch into new growth areas.

Many companies recognize the value of giving and receiving feedback. Probably one of the best-known companies to embody this is Netflix, which frames this in its Culture Memo as having candor. Their latest Culture Memo (updated in 2024) refers to this value as being "willing to receive and give feedback," being "open about what's working and what needs to improve," and admitting mistakes openly and sharing learnings widely.

Having worked at Netflix, I remember the importance of feedback. And although giving feedback may feel uncomfortable, receiving it with grace and with positive intention may be even more difficult. But it's absolutely necessary, in order to understand yourself. Sure, in the working context, feedback is often embedded as a performance tool, but when you embody it as an individual, it becomes even more powerful.

I remember a pivotal moment when a colleague pulled me aside one day and asked,

"You're doing a great job managing your responsibilities but if you were aiming higher, what challenges would you take on?"

That question stopped me in my tracks. I realized I hadn't thought about what "the next level" looked like for me. I'd been so focused on doing my current job well that I hadn't considered how I could expand my skills or push myself in new directions.

Feedback like this is more than just critique. It's an invitation to reimagine our potential. Sometimes, it's an encouraging nudge.

"You're doing well here, but have you thought about taking on more strategic projects?"

Other times, it's a tough question that prompts deeper reflection.

"Are you learning something new, or are you just repeating what you already know?"

Each comment or question has the power to shake us out of routine and inspire us to move forward with intention.

Activity 3 360-Degree Reflection

Ask a trusted peer, mentor, or supervisor for their honest perspective on your work. Consider asking them questions like:

- *What do you think is my greatest strength?*
- *Where do you see room for me to grow or challenge myself more?*
- *Are there areas where you think I could be using my skills differently?*

Take time to reflect on the feedback you receive, and note any patterns or themes. Choose one piece of advice or insight that resonates and think about a way to incorporate it into your work in the coming weeks. This exercise isn't just about improvement. It's about uncovering potential paths forward that align with your strengths and aspirations.

Set a Bold Goal: Setting a bold goal, one that stretches you and makes you a little uncomfortable, can reignite your drive and shift your perspective on what's possible. Bold goals are powerful because they disrupt the routines we've become accustomed to and challenge us to grow in new ways.

They require courage, creativity, and a willingness to move beyond the familiar. In fact, I've devoted an entire chapter to living boldly, so take a look at Chapter 4 for more on this topic.

A bold goal might mean going after a leadership role you're not entirely sure you're ready for or pivoting to a different industry where you're forced to learn a new language of skills and ideas. It could mean launching a side project. Bold goals shake us out of complacency and remind us of our capacity for growth.

I remember when I decided to set the goal of leading a cross-functional team.

It was daunting.

I had always been comfortable in roles where my expertise was clear and I knew the landscape. But suddenly, I was managing people from entirely different backgrounds, each with their perspectives, skills, and ways of working.

Leading this team meant learning to adapt, listen in new ways, and let go of needing all the answers. It was messy, often unpredictable, and sometimes exhausting, but it gave me a renewed sense of purpose. And for the first time, I felt like I was learning, stretching, and building something meaningful.

Here's another example of what it's like to set a bold goal. When I met Lee, she was at a crossroads. Her career in governance and compliance was stellar, built on a foundation of diligence, precision, and unshakable integrity. But beneath that solid exterior, Lee felt a growing restlessness. She had mastered her craft, but the question lingered: *What's next?*

Lee had a bold, almost audacious dream: she wanted to become the #1 global leader in her field. She envisioned a role where she could influence not just policies but the entire trajectory of an organization. It was a leap that felt as thrilling as it did impossible. The weight of that ambition sat heavy on her shoulders. Could she really step out of her current role and into the global spotlight?

At first, the enormity of her goal was paralyzing. The world of global leadership seemed light-years away from the detail-oriented, rule-bound world she had mastered. Stepping into strategic conversations with senior executives felt daunting. Questions like *What if I fail?* and *What if I don't belong?* loomed large, and self-doubt crept in.

But Lee didn't back down. Together, we worked on breaking her big goal into smaller, actionable steps. She started by immersing herself in global business trends, attending leadership forums, and studying how top executives shaped strategy and influenced change. Slowly but steadily, she began to see patterns and opportunities she hadn't noticed before.

She also leaned into her strengths. Her diligence, once confined to compliance, became her secret weapon in strategic discussions. While others skimmed the surface, Lee brought depth and foresight, earning her a reputation as a voice of clarity and insight. Bit by bit, she started to shift how she saw herself, not just as a diligent executor but as a leader with a seat at the table.

There were tough moments, of course. Some meetings left her feeling small, as though she'd stumbled into a foreign language of high-level strategy. But she kept showing up, asking questions, and learning. Each step forward, no matter how small, fueled her confidence.

Over time, her vision began to take shape. Senior leaders noticed her ability to connect the dots and foresee risks others missed. They started asking for her opinion, inviting her to join broader strategic conversations. Lee wasn't just part of the room. She was shaping it.

Lee's journey is still unfolding, but the transformation is undeniable. She's gone from wondering *what's next* to boldly charting a path toward global leadership. Her story is a testament to the power of setting a goal so big it scares you, and then showing up, day after day, to make it a reality.

Activity 4 Set Your Bold Goal

Take a moment to consider a goal that excites and challenges you, something beyond your comfort zone that would push you into new territory. Reflect on the following questions:

- *What's a goal that would stretch me to learn something new or take on greater responsibility?*
- *If I could achieve anything in my career, what one goal would bring me closer to that vision?*

Write down your bold goal, then outline one small step you will take this week to move toward it. Whether scheduling a conversation with someone who is doing something similar, researching a new skill, or volunteering for a project outside your usual role, even the smallest action will build momentum toward realizing your goal.

Expand Your Network: Expanding your network beyond the usual circles can be one of the most transformative actions you take in your career. Connecting with people from different fields, industries, or backgrounds brings fresh perspectives, new ideas, and unexpected opportunities.

Often, it's a single, meaningful conversation that opens up a whole new direction you hadn't considered. Whether attending industry events, joining a professional group, or simply reaching out to someone you admire, each interaction can lead to insights and inspiration that break you out of your current path and help you see new possibilities.

Building relationships outside your comfort zone requires courage and openness, but the rewards can be life changing. Each new connection can offer knowledge, encouragement, or an idea that could shift your trajectory entirely.

I met Priya, who had been working as a technical writer for several years, creating documentation, user guides, and support materials for a software company, some years ago. While she valued the importance of her role in helping users understand the product, she felt limited in her ability to influence how the product was built and used.

Priya was curious about design and user experience but wasn't sure how to make a career shift. At a conference, she struck up a conversation with a senior product designer during a lunch break. Their discussion about design thinking and user empathy sparked something in her, and she asked if they could meet again to continue the conversation. Over coffee, Priya gained insights into the role of a product designer, learning how the team works closely with users to shape intuitive and valuable experiences.

Inspired, Priya took a design thinking course and began volunteering to help the design team with small projects in her current job. She contributed by writing content from a user-centered perspective and bringing her insights to design discussions. Over time, her experience and new skills opened doors, and she successfully transitioned into a junior role in product design. This change reconnected her with a sense of purpose and creativity she hadn't felt in years.

Activity 5 Networking Challenge

Identify one person you admire or would like to learn from outside your immediate circle. This could be someone in a different role, industry, or field that piques your interest. Reach out for a brief chat, whether virtual or in person, and prepare a few thoughtful questions. After the conversation, reflect on your insights and consider how they might influence your career path. Note any ideas that came up, and if the conversation sparked a new interest or goal, consider taking a small step to explore it further.

Revisit Your Values: Sometimes, career stagnation is a sign that we've drifted away from what truly matters to us. When our work no longer aligns with our core values, even the most accomplished roles can start to feel empty. Taking time to reconnect with your values is a powerful way to rekindle a sense of purpose and bring meaning back into your career.

Reflective practices, like journaling or quiet contemplation, can provide clarity on what you want from your work and life. By realigning with your values, you may discover not only what's missing but also how to steer your career in a direction that feels genuinely fulfilling.

I remember my friend's husband, David, working in a fast-paced consulting firm for nearly a decade. He often traveled, spending weeks away from home and working late to meet demanding client expectations. But when he became a father, he started to feel the weight of his job's toll on his family life. He missed seeing his kids grow up, and the sacrifice began to feel too great. During a weekend retreat, David took some time to reflect and journal, realizing that his core values had shifted. Family and work-life balance, which he'd once overlooked in pursuit of success, were now at the forefront.

This realization led him to make a bold decision: he left his consulting role and took a position in a local company that valued flexibility. The new role came with its own challenges, but David found immense fulfillment in being able to share family dinners, attend his children's school events, and still contribute meaningfully at work. Reconnecting with his values helped him design a career that felt genuinely aligned.

Going back to your core values is a helpful first step when you're thinking about what lights you up. But it can also feel daunting when someone says "what are your core values?." Figure 1.1 contains a variety of values that can help you get started. These words are not just abstract concepts. They're the foundation of what drives you, shapes your decisions, and gives meaning to your work. Values like integrity, creativity, growth, or connection can act as your personal compass, helping you navigate through uncertainty and prioritize what truly matters.

If the idea of pinpointing your core values feels overwhelming, start by reflecting on moments in your life when you've felt truly fulfilled or deeply frustrated. What was present in those moments (or glaringly absent)? For example, if you felt energized leading a team to achieve a shared goal, cooperation or leadership might be a core value for you. If frustration often stems from feeling stifled in rigid environments, freedom or excitement could be guiding principles.

Remember that values aren't just static labels that evolve as you grow and change. Revisiting them regularly can provide clarity during periods of transition or uncertainty. They're a tool, not a test. Use them to reconnect

Accountability, Accuracy, Achievement, Adventurousness, Altruism, Ambition, Assertiveness, Balance, Being the best, Belonging, Boldness, Calmness, Carefulness, Challenge, Cheerfulness, Clear-mindedness, Commitment, Community, Compassion, Competitiveness, Connection, Consistency, Contentment, Continuous Improvement, Contribution, Control, Cooperation, Correctness, Courtesy, Creativity, Curiosity, Decisiveness, Democraticness, Dependability, Determination, Devoutness, Diligence, Discipline, Discretion, Diversity, Dynamism, Economy, Effectiveness, Efficiency, Elegance, Empathy, Enjoyment, Enthusiasm, Equality, Excellence, Excitement, Expertise, Exploration, Expressiveness, Fairness, Faith, Family-orientedness, Fitness, Fluency, Focus, Freedom, Fun, Generosity, Goodness, Grace, Growth, Happiness, Hard work, Health, Helping society, Holiness, Honesty, Honor, Humility, Independence, Ingenuity, Inner harmony, Inquisitiveness, Insightfulness, Intelligence, Intellectual status, Integrity, Intuition, Joy, Justice, Leadership, Legacy, Love, Loyalty, Making a difference, Mastery, Merit, Obedience, Openness, Order, Originality, Patriotism, Perfection, Piety, Positivity, Practicality, Preparedness, Professionalism, Prudence, Quality-orientation, Reliability, Resourcefulness, Restraint, Results-oriented, Rigor, Security, Self-actualization, Self-control, Selflessness, Self-reliance, Sensitivity, Serenity, Service, Shrewdness, Simplicity, Soundness, Speed, Spontaneity, Stability, Strategic, Strength, Structure, Success, Support, Teamwork, Temperance, Thankfulness, Thoroughness, Thoughtfulness, Timeliness, Tolerance, Traditionalism, Trustworthiness, Truth-seeking, Understanding, Uniqueness, Unity, Usefulness, Vision, Vitality.

Figure 1.1 Core Values.

with what lights you up and to evaluate whether your current path aligns with the life you want to create.

Once you've identified a few values that resonate, try integrating them into your decision-making process. Ask yourself: *How does this choice honor my values? Does this opportunity align with what I stand for?* When you use your values as a filter, you'll find it easier to choose paths that feel authentic and fulfilling, even when the way forward isn't entirely clear.

Activity 6 Values Check-In

Spend ten minutes journaling about your core values. Start by reflecting on the following:

- *What values have guided my career decisions so far?*
- *Are my current role and projects aligned with what I truly care about?*
- *What aspects of my work bring me the most satisfaction or dissatisfaction, and how do they connect with my values?*

If you find that your current role isn't aligned with your values, identify one small way you could bring these values into your daily work, even if it's a small shift. For instance, if connection is a value, maybe you can reach out to colleagues for collaborative projects. If creativity is important, consider seeking out more innovative assignments or side projects.

Take Action, No Matter How Small

The path out of stagnation often begins with the smallest of steps. When you feel stuck, taking even tiny, almost unnoticeable actions can help you regain momentum and find a renewed sense of purpose.

It might be as simple as updating your LinkedIn profile, sending a message to an old friend or mentor, or signing up for a workshop.

What matters isn't the size of the action but the intention behind it. Each small step builds upon the last, creating a ripple effect that can gradually shift your trajectory in profound ways.

Taking these first steps is often the most challenging part. They can feel inconsequential in the moment, but together, they create a momentum that leads to real change.

I knew Carlos, who had spent years in finance, managing budgets and analyzing cost reports. He'd always been passionate about the environment, and in recent years, climate change had weighed heavily on his mind.

One day, he was scrolling through LinkedIn and came across an article on environmental policy and how financial expertise could play a role in sustainability initiatives. Inspired, he decided to explore further.

Carlos registered for a webinar to learn more about climate change and how companies were achieving their environmental goals. He told himself it was just for personal enrichment, but the material was so intriguing that he found himself staying up late to dive deeper into topics like carbon credits. Over time, he began to see how his financial skills could be applied to environmental initiatives.

Carlos spoke to his manager about the possibility of working on sustainability projects within his company. Impressed by his enthusiasm, his manager offered him the opportunity to explore eco-friendly budgeting practices. This gave Carlos a renewed sense of purpose, blending his financial background with his personal values. Today, he's on a meaningful path aligned with his passion for environmental impact – all thanks to that first small step of signing up for a webinar.

Activity 7 Small Steps Forward

Take a moment to think about one small action that aligns with the change you're seeking. This could be as simple as:

- Sending a message to someone you'd like to learn from.
- Updating your resume or LinkedIn profile.
- Registering for an introductory course in an area of interest.
- Reading an article on a new skill or field.

Identify this small action, then take it today. Don't focus on the result. Appreciate that you're initiating forward momentum. Notice how this small step makes you feel, and consider if there is another step you could take tomorrow. Sometimes, change starts not with giant leaps but with quiet, consistent forward motion.

The Cost of Staying Stuck

Remaining in a rut exacts a toll, not just on your career but on your entire sense of well-being. Prolonged dissatisfaction in your work can gradually chip away at your energy, engagement, and physical health.

When we're unfulfilled at work, the impact often spills over into our personal lives, affecting our relationships, our sense of purpose, and our overall happiness.

Career stagnation doesn't resolve independently. It takes intentional, sometimes uncomfortable, action to break free. Recognizing this cost can be the wake-up call that prompts you to realign and move toward a path that truly feels like yours. You can ask yourself questions like:

When was the last time I felt genuinely challenged and excited by my work?

Am I doing what truly fulfills me, or simply what I've become good at?

What small, actionable step could I take today to stretch beyond my comfort zone?

Each question invites you to confront the reality of where you are and imagine where you could be if you began moving forward, even in the smallest of ways. Consider them as first steps, guiding you toward a career that nourishes, rather than drains your sense of purpose.

A Moment of Courage

Recognizing that you're stuck is a powerful revelation. It's a moment of honesty, a quiet acknowledgment that you're ready for something more from your career and life.

You've taken that courageous first step by identifying the signs of stagnation, and in doing so, you've begun to reconnect with what truly matters. It takes courage to admit when something isn't working, especially when it looks good on the surface. But now you know the cost of staying in place, and you're ready to explore what could be possible if you moved with intention.

In this chapter, we've uncovered the importance of self-awareness and reconnecting with your core values. We've explored how even the smallest actions, whether it's setting a bold goal, expanding your network, or realigning with your deepest values, can start to build momentum.

Each step forward, no matter how small, declares your commitment to a career that truly reflects who you are and what you aspire to achieve.

But knowing you're ready to break free is only the beginning.

The true transformation comes when you turn that awareness into meaningful, intentional action. In the next chapter, we'll explore the critical shift required to move forward and how to adopt a mindset that allows you to step beyond the familiar and embrace growth.

We'll dive into practical strategies to reframe your thinking, challenge assumptions, and lay the foundation for a career and a life that fulfills you. You're standing at the edge of something extraordinary, and it's time to step forward, one purposeful choice at a time.

Notes

1 Abele, A. E., J. Volmer, and D. Spurk. 2012. "Career Stagnation: Underlying Dilemmas and Solutions in Contemporary Work Environments." *Work and Quality of Life: Ethical Practices in Organizations*, edited by N. P. Reilly, M. J. Sirgy, and C. A. Gorman, 107–132. Springer. https://doi.org/10.1007/978-94-007-4059-4_7.
2 Sutin, A. R., M. Luchetti, Y. Stephan, A. A. Sesker, and A. Terracciano. 2024. "Purpose in Life and Stress: An Individual-Participant Meta-Analysis of 16 Samples." *Journal of Affective Disorders* 345: 378–385. https://doi.org/10.1016/j.jad.2023.10.149.
3 Amabile, Teresa M., and Steven J. Kramer. 2011. *The Power of Small Wins*. Harvard Business Review Press.
4 World Health Organization. 2019. "Burn-out an 'Occupational Phenomenon': International Classification of Diseases." *WHO*, May 28. https://www.who.int/news/item/28-05-2019-burn-out-an-occupational-phenomenon-international-classification-of-diseases.
5 Tupper, H., and S. Ellis. 2021. "Make Learning a Part of Your Daily Routine." *Harvard Business Review*, November. https://hbr.org/2021/11/make-learning-a-part-of-your-daily-routine.

Chapter 2

Beyond the Comfort Zone

"Sorry, Megan, but this is just the way things are."

I can't count how many times I've heard that. It might come from a well-meaning mentor, a seasoned colleague, or even that small, doubtful voice within myself. The idea was always the same: maybe I shouldn't push so hard to question the rules, to challenge the system. I'd hear it when I tried to suggest a new approach or saw a chance to improve something that had been "working" for years. Each time, it felt like a quiet dismissal, a reminder that my eagerness to grow was just a little out of place in the status quo.

But deep down, I knew there had to be more. I felt restless and hungry for progress that went beyond the ordinary expectations of my role. I realized that to reach my potential, I needed to rethink how I approached challenges, risks, and even failures. Even if it meant challenging my own mindset, moving past the boundaries of what I already knew, and embracing growth as a process that thrives on discomfort and courage.

In Chapter 1, we explored those early signs that tell us it's time for a change. Now, we're going to take it a step further. This chapter is about that crucial shift that allows you to transform feelings of dissatisfaction into a roadmap for growth. Adopting a growth mindset isn't just about thinking positively but cultivating a perspective that sees every challenge as an invitation to learn, every setback as a lesson, and every day as an opportunity to stretch a little further.

If you've ever felt boxed in by the need to stay in your lane, to avoid risks for fear of failing, or to limit yourself to only what you're good at, this chapter is for you. We're going to look at what it means to embrace a mindset that doesn't just accept change but actively seeks it.

Understanding the Growth Mindset

In her groundbreaking book, *Mindset*,[1] psychologist Dr. Carol Dweck introduced a concept that has reshaped how we view success: the *growth*

DOI: 10.4324/9781003627265-3

mindset. Dweck explains that people generally adopt one of two perspectives on their abilities.

With a **fixed mindset**, individuals see their abilities as static, which can lead them to avoid challenges, give up quickly, and interpret effort as a sign of inadequacy.

However, a **growth mindset** is rooted in the belief that abilities can be developed through learning, effort, and resilience. People with a growth mindset embrace challenges, persevere through obstacles, and view failures as valuable learning experiences.

The science behind this concept is compelling. Neuroscientists have shown that the brain is capable of change, a phenomenon known as *neuroplasticity*. This means you can physically rewire neural pathways with effort and the right mindset, enabling growth, resilience, and learning.

Researchers[2] found that people who embraced a growth mindset activated brain regions critical for adaptive learning and resilience. These areas are associated with higher-order functions like problem-solving, cognitive flexibility, and persistence. In other words, you can approach obstacles with an open mind, adapt strategies as needed, and remain motivated even when faced with setbacks.

Conversely, those with a fixed mindset displayed increased activation in the amygdala, the brain's center for processing fear and threat. This activation triggered avoidance behaviors when faced with challenges, reinforcing a cycle of self-doubt and stagnation. The amygdala's response in fixed-mindset individuals suggests they may perceive effort and difficulty as threats to their self-image, leading them to shy away from challenging tasks that could otherwise foster growth.

This neuroscientific evidence underscores the transformative power of a growth mindset. And understanding this science reveals that, no matter how stuck you may feel, you can shift your mindset to reframe challenges as opportunities.

Why High Achievers Struggle with Mindset Shifts

You might think that knowing about the growth mindset would make it easy to adopt. But ironically, high achievers often find this shift particularly difficult. This challenge is known as the **Success Trap**, which I introduced in Chapter 1. The very strategies that drive initial success (perfectionism, control, and risk avoidance) can later become barriers to growth.

In my early career, I thrived on being the expert and avoided mistakes at all costs. But over time, I realized I'd become confined by my own success.

I stopped taking risks, avoided challenges outside my comfort zone, and stayed within the safe boundaries of my expertise. And I convinced myself that it was the right thing to have a Plan A, Plan B, and Plan C for the initiatives my team deployed, rather than appreciating that failure and experimentation were actually the path to growth.

This is often true for those of us who have jobs where our impact is tied to success and especially external success metrics. Our annual bonus. Potential promotion. Being considered for stretch assignments or projects. Even though our companies encourage innovation and risk-taking, is it really rewarded?

So for me, instead of growing, I was stagnating.

I found that it took a lot of courage to move outside of those safe boundaries. After all, it felt good to be known as *that* person who would deliver results, build high-performing teams, and go above and beyond. Those treasured results were great for my annual performance review and my resume. I'm sure you know what I'm talking about. *Who wants to be the one that isn't successful?*

It took a senior executive one day to point out that my goals weren't pushing me hard enough, for me to change my way of thinking. He actually said that the way he viewed goals was that he was *expecting* that I would fail on at least 20% of them, otherwise I hadn't set myself difficult enough challenges.

What?

I felt both exposed and uncertain. *Was this even real?* Surely it was a trap, I thought. Designed to prove that I couldn't deliver results (ah, my fixed mindset was taking over my thoughts).

After all, I'd spent years building a reputation as a reliable problem-solver, the one who could be trusted to get things right. But I hadn't realized how much I was holding myself back by staying in safe territory.

I was choosing what I knew over what I could learn, trading growth for a sense of security.

Deciding to change that was unsettling.

I took on challenges that were unfamiliar, and I couldn't predict the outcome. At times, I found myself second-guessing, grappling with self-doubt as I faced situations that tested skills I wasn't yet confident in.

Yet, as I leaned into these new experiences, I discovered a different kind of satisfaction. Each step revealed strengths I hadn't tapped into before, and instead of staying within what I already knew, I was embracing what I was still becoming.

Dr. Brené Brown, a leading scholar on vulnerability explains what was happening.[3] You see, high achievers often feel the pressure to maintain a facade of competence. This fear of not measuring up, known as **Imposter Syndrome,** can cause even the most accomplished professionals to shy away from challenges.

But vulnerability is essential for growth. You unlock profound personal and professional development when you allow yourself to be challenged, not to have all the answers, and to embrace potential failure.

This insight reminded me of a moment early in my career when I was invited to join a team evaluating an acquisition. This task felt far beyond my expertise. I don't have an MBA, and I didn't have a clue what I was supposed to do. I threw myself into the process by reviewing financial reports, analyzing operational strengths and weaknesses, and spending long hours in the data room before joining more experienced colleagues on the site visits.

Immersed in a sea of complex information, I pushed myself to understand the nuances, asking countless questions and seeking clarity on every detail. The pressure to keep up was intense, and at times, I questioned whether I was in over my head.

But I chose to lean into the challenge, admitting when I didn't have all the answers and learning from my teammates' expertise. That openness was initially intimidating, yet it fostered a deeper trust within the team, allowing us to collaborate effectively and grow together through the process.

Activity 8 Identify and Stretch Beyond Your Success Traps

To break free from the habits that may limit your growth, take small steps to stretch beyond your comfort zone.

1 **Identify Success Traps**
List one or two habits that have contributed to your success but may limit growth, for example:

- *Perfectionism*: Avoiding tasks if they can't be done perfectly.
- *Control*: Reluctance to delegate or let go.
- *Risk Avoidance*: Sticking to familiar projects over new challenges.

2 **Choose One to Stretch:** Pick one habit to challenge this week. Take a small action that steps beyond it:

- Aim to complete a task with minor imperfections.
- Delegate a task without overseeing every detail.
- Commit to one project outside your comfort zone.

3 **Reflect and Reframe:** At the end of the week, journal briefly: What did you learn about adapting and letting go?

Rewiring Your Mindset

Shifting from a fixed mindset to a growth mindset requires intentional, consistent effort. This transformation, known as **cognitive reframing**, involves replacing limiting beliefs with growth-oriented perspectives. Let's explore how you can start this shift:

Recognize Your Fixed Mindset Triggers

The first step to breaking free from a fixed mindset is learning to identify the moments when it sneaks into your thoughts and actions. These moments might feel heavy, even laden with fear, doubt, or comparison, but they are also opportunities for transformation.

One of the habits I've adopted for myself is to ask myself *How do you feel?* and label the feeling. I will confess that this has been difficult for me. I would prefer to bulldoze my way through situations rather than sit in the moment and reflect on my feelings. I've had many years' experience of being the composed executive who moved from one situation or crisis to the next. But putting a word to the feeling has made it manageable and less overwhelming.

It's given the emotion structure, allowing me to face it directly instead of letting it simmer beneath the surface. By naming the feeling, whether it's fear, frustration, self-doubt, or even envy, I can begin to understand it and make sense of why it's there.

For example, when I've felt the sting of comparison, labeling it as envy has helped me recognize what that emotion is pointing to. It's often a sign that there's something I admire or aspire to, in someone else's success. Rather than letting it pull me into self-doubt, I use it as an opportunity to ask, *What can I learn from this? What steps can I take to work toward a similar achievement?*

This practice doesn't eliminate the emotions entirely (believe me, they are still there), but it reduces their intensity and gives me a way to respond with intention rather than reaction. It shifts the focus from *Why do I feel this way?* to *What can I do about it?*

By bringing awareness to my feelings, I can begin to see them as signals that guide me, rather than barriers that hold me back.

If you're wondering about the type of fixed mindset triggers that high achievers often experience, here's a few:

Avoiding Challenges Due to Fear of Failure: Think about the times you've hesitated to say yes to a new opportunity. Maybe it was a role that felt just out of reach or a project where the stakes seemed too high. That fear, you know the one that whispers *What if I fail? What will people think?*, is a hallmark of a fixed mindset. It convinces you that failure isn't an option, and in doing so, it robs you of the chance to grow. Recognizing this avoidance is powerful. What if, instead of fearing failure, you saw challenges as a playground for discovery?

Focusing on Proving Competence Instead of Embracing Learning: There's a subtle pressure many of us feel: the need to prove we belong, to show we're capable, to never let others see us struggle. It's the reason you might find yourself over-preparing for a meeting or clinging to the safety of what you already know. This mindset traps you in a loop of validation, where your energy is spent on being impressive instead of being curious. Imagine the freedom of releasing that pressure and diving into situations with the sole aim of learning. No, not to look good, but to *become* good.

Giving Up Easily After Encountering Obstacles: We all know the disappointment of hitting a roadblock, whether it's a failed attempt, a missed opportunity, or unexpected criticism. For some, it feels like proof of inadequacy, a signal to retreat. But what if obstacles weren't roadblocks but launchpads? When you give up too quickly, you deny yourself the chance to build resilience and discover what you're truly capable of.

Feeling Threatened by Others' Success: Seeing someone else excel can sometimes feel like a mirror reflecting your own insecurities. Their success might make you question your path, your abilities, or even your worth. But this mindset isolates you, turning potential allies and mentors into competitors. What if, instead, you viewed their success as a source of inspiration or even a path showing what's possible and a reminder that growth is contagious?

Every time you notice these triggers, pause. Feel the pull of your thoughts and ask yourself: *Am I acting out of fear, or am I opening myself to growth?* That pause, even if it's brief, is where transformation begins. It's the moment you reclaim your power and choose curiosity over comfort, progress over perfection, and growth over stagnation.

I've worked with a lot of exceptional operations leaders. These are leaders on the front line, often managing large teams with complex environments, challenging targets, and a lot of daily unknowns.

Hazel was one of the best people-focused operations managers I'd ever worked with. She empowered her team to take ownership, encouraged collaborative problem-solving, and consistently built a positive, high-performing team culture. Her leadership style allowed her team to operate smoothly, even under pressure, and she just knew when to support her team. However, after years of focusing on team empowerment and day-to-day operations, Hazel confided in me that she felt ready to make a broader impact. She wanted to move from solely managing people to influencing the company's strategic direction.

But, taking on a strategic role was intimidating. It meant shifting from empowering her team's daily work to considering how those efforts fit into the company's long-term vision. Joining higher-level discussions and presenting her insights to senior leaders felt outside her comfort zone, and at times, she wondered if she was too focused on her team to think big picture.

To overcome these doubts, Hazel reframed her mindset. She saw that her strength in people management could actually support her in a strategic role by helping her understand the needs of employees at every level. She started engaging in leadership training focused on strategic thinking, seeking feedback from senior leaders, and gradually stepping into roles that required her to consider the bigger picture. Over time, she gained confidence in balancing her people-centered approach with a strategic perspective, contributing valuable insights to the company's vision. By embracing growth, Hazel transformed from a trusted people manager into a strategic leader, ultimately creating a greater impact for both her team and her organization.

Challenge Your Fixed Mindset

Once you've recognized the moments when your fixed mindset takes hold, the real work begins: questioning the beliefs that fuel those triggers. These beliefs often feel deeply ingrained, almost like truths, because they've shaped how you've approached challenges, setbacks, and successes for years. But here's the powerful realization. They are not facts. They are stories you've told yourself.

And stories can be rewritten.

Challenging these beliefs can feel uncomfortable, even daunting. You're going to need to peel back layers of fear, self-doubt, and comparison to uncover what is really driving your reactions. But this process is where transformation begins. By examining these thoughts and holding them up to the light, you can start to see them for what they are: assumptions, not absolutes.

Here are some prompts to help you break free from the grip of your fixed mindset:

- **"What am I afraid will happen if I fail?"** Often, the fear of failure is trying to protect your self-worth or avoid judgment. But what if failure wasn't the end, but a step in the process? Ask yourself, *If failure is inevitable in learning, how can I reframe it as feedback instead of a reflection of my ability?*
- **"What evidence do I have that this belief is true?"** Fixed mindset beliefs thrive on exaggeration. You might tell yourself, *I'm just not good at this* or *I'll never be able to figure it out,* but are those statements grounded in fact? Challenge the validity of these thoughts by seeking out instances where you have succeeded, learned, or grown in similar situations.

- **"What would I say to a friend in this situation?"** The words you use with yourself often lack the kindness and encouragement you would offer to someone else. Imagine a friend sharing the same doubts you're experiencing. How would you respond to them? Use that perspective to shift the tone of your inner dialogue.
- **"What am I missing by staying in my comfort zone?"** Fixed mindsets love comfort zones, but growth happens on the edges of discomfort. Reflect on the opportunities, experiences, or skills you might be passing up because of a fear of the unknown. Imagine the person you could become by stepping into that space, even if it feels uncertain.
- **"How can I focus on the process instead of the outcome?"** A fixed mindset is obsessed with results. Shift your attention to the process instead. Ask yourself, *What can I learn from this experience? How can I grow, even if the outcome isn't perfect?*

This process isn't about eliminating doubt or fear entirely. It's about meeting those feelings with curiosity and courage, giving yourself permission to see challenges as opportunities rather than threats. Some of the best teams I've ever worked with always explored challenges with curiosity.

As Amazon says in its 16 leadership principles[4]:

> Leaders are never done learning and always seek to improve themselves. They are curious about new possibilities and act to explore them.

The more you practice questioning your fixed mindset, the weaker its hold becomes. Each time you challenge those ingrained beliefs, you take a step closer to unlocking your potential and the version of yourself you're striving to become.

Activity 9 Challenge Your Beliefs

1. **Identify a Limiting Belief:** Think of a recent time you hesitated to try something new. Write down the belief holding you back (e.g., "I'm not tech-savvy enough").
2. **Ask Yourself:**
    - Does this belief help or hinder my growth?
    - What advice would I give a friend in this situation?
    - How can I see this as a learning opportunity?
3. **Reframe It:** Rewrite the belief positively (e.g., "Learning tech skills is a chance to grow"). Take one small action this week to test it.

Focus on Learning Over Approval

One of the most transformative shifts you can make in developing a growth mindset is moving from seeking approval to prioritizing your personal development. For many of us, the need for validation runs deep. It's a natural human desire to be recognized, to feel competent, and to be seen as capable in the eyes of others.

But this need can become a trap, tethering your self-worth to external applause rather than your own progress. Shifting the focus to learning (your growth, your curiosity, and your development) can unlock a new level of resilience and fulfillment. A Michigan State University study[5] highlights how people with a growth mindset are more likely to embrace challenges and persist through setbacks.

Why?

Because they view these experiences as opportunities to expand their abilities rather than as tests of their worth. This shift from *proving yourself* to *improving yourself* changes the way you approach your goals, your challenges, and even your failures.

Making this change requires intentionality. You need to redefine what success looks like and understand that success is not a flawless performance but meaningful progress. Here's how to start:

Set Learning Goals Instead of Performance Goals: Performance goals often sound like, *I need to ace this presentation,* or *I have to deliver a perfect outcome.* These goals focus on external validation and leave little room for experimentation or mistakes. Remember we talked earlier about how we often feel stuck with outcome or success goals, especially when they are linked to things like a bonus or promotion.

A learning goal, however, reframes the same situation: *I want to explore a new communication technique* or *I'll practice engaging more with my audience.* By shifting the focus to what you can gain from the experience, you open the door to growth and take the pressure off the need to be perfect. And sure, learning goals can be a little more difficult to measure than performance goals, but give it a try and see how it works out for you.

Seek Feedback as a Tool for Growth: Feedback can feel intimidating, especially when you're striving for approval. But constructive feedback is one of the most valuable tools for improvement. Rather than fearing it, view it as a gift that provides insights you might not see on your own. When you stop equating feedback with judgment, it becomes a way to refine your skills and move closer to your potential.

Redefine Your Relationship with Mistakes: Mistakes aren't failures. They're data points. What would happen if you looked at the data objectively? Chances are, it would offer valuable lessons that can inform your future efforts. When you prioritize learning, mistakes will give you less of a stomach ache because they're no longer personal. They're simply part of the process.

This shift from approval to learning isn't always easy. It requires letting go of the need to always "get it right" and embracing the vulnerability of imperfection. But in doing so, you'll find yourself growing in ways you never imagined. Your confidence will no longer be tied to fleeting moments of recognition but will be rooted in the knowledge that you're constantly evolving.

Activity 10 Shift from Approval to Learning Goals

To help reframe your focus from approval to growth, try this quick exercise:

1. **Identify a Goal You Currently Have:** Think of a current goal where you're aiming for approval or perfection (e.g., delivering a flawless presentation or impressing a senior leader).
2. **Reframe as a Learning Goal:** Rewrite the goal focusing on personal growth. For example:
   - Original Goal: "Deliver a perfect presentation."
   - Learning Goal: "Try a new storytelling technique in my presentation to engage the audience."
3. **Plan for Feedback:** Commit to seeking constructive feedback after completing the task. Ask specific questions like, *What could I improve?* or *How did this new approach come across?*
4. **Reflect:** At the end, journal your experience. What did you learn from focusing on growth instead of approval? How did it feel to shift your focus?

This exercise helps you practice setting goals, prioritizing learning and growth, and allowing you to embrace the process without seeking validation.

Building Growth-Oriented Habits

The Power of Stacked Wins

I'm not sure where the concept of **stacked wins** originated, but it's something I learned from a previous manager, who among other things, had been the President of Gatorade. A talented and seasoned operator, he had one of the biggest impacts in my career in terms of thinking about how to compound results, or stacking wins.

After all, adopting a growth mindset is one thing, but sustaining it requires intentional, growth-oriented habits. These practices act as a foundation, keeping you focused on learning and progress even when challenges arise, ultimately building small, consistent actions that accumulate into meaningful growth over time.

When a senior leader first challenged me to broaden my perspective, I didn't realize she was guiding me toward a growth habit I hadn't yet developed: connecting my insights to the organization's larger goals. I had spent years refining my expertise in safety, focusing on compliance and risk management, and I took pride in delivering reliable results. But she saw potential in me beyond my safety expertise and believed I could influence the organization in ways I hadn't yet considered.

Our conversation was a turning point. She looked me right in the eye and said, "You're more than a safety leader. You understand how people and processes intersect across the organization. I want you to bring that perspective to the leadership team, not just the safety numbers, but the larger picture they contribute to."

At first, I resisted. "I'm here because I know safety. I'm not a strategist or a finance expert."

But she pressed on.

"Leadership isn't only about expertise. It's about influence and vision. You have a unique perspective on how our culture, our people, and our systems shape our results. We need that voice in the room."

Feeling uncertain and vulnerable, I wondered how I could contribute meaningfully beyond my specific expertise. But she gave me a simple framework to start with: each time I prepared my safety insights, I'd connect them to a broader outcome.

For example, instead of simply saying, "We need more training to improve safety," I could reframe it as, "Investing in training boosts engagement and productivity, reducing incidents and supporting our long-term goals." This small step was my first "stacked win" toward building influence beyond my defined role.

Over time, these stacked wins began to build momentum. Each time I reframed my insights, I felt a bit more confident and comfortable stepping into conversations about broader impacts. By connecting safety to company goals, I discovered I could contribute to the bigger picture, influencing productivity, culture, and even strategy. These small adjustments in my approach began to stack, creating a cumulative effect that amplified my impact.

This experience taught me that building growth-oriented habits isn't about instant mastery or grand gestures, but taking small, steady steps that stack over time, each one building on the last. Leadership, as I learned, isn't just about operating within the boundaries of what we know; it's about expanding those boundaries to find new ways to make a meaningful difference.

As I began to reframe my contributions and connect them to broader goals, I realized that growth-oriented habits weren't just about what I shared in meetings. They also extended how I responded to feedback and adjusted along the way.

Embracing feedback, including welcoming constructive insights and using them as fuel for growth, became the next habit I needed to develop. This practice pushed me to examine my blind spots, refine my approach, and continually expand my leadership capacity.

Embracing Feedback

We talked earlier about taking feedback as a gift, and how many companies view feedback as an integral part of their culture.

Let's speak some hard truths, though.

Feedback can be uncomfortable, especially when it touches areas we think we've mastered. But leaders with a growth mindset understand that feedback is one of the most valuable tools for ongoing improvement.

In their book, *Thanks for the Feedback*,[6] Dr. Sheila Heen and Dr. Douglas Stone say that people who actively embrace constructive criticism grow more, adapt faster, and ultimately perform at a higher level than those who shy away from it. Instead of seeing feedback as a personal critique, leaders with a growth mindset view it as an essential guide to mastery.

To make the most of feedback, it helps to approach it as a structured habit. Here are ways to build this habit into your leadership practice:

Regularly Seek Feedback from Colleagues, Mentors, or Team Members: Instead of waiting for formal reviews, take the initiative to seek feedback regularly. Ask colleagues and mentors for their honest impressions, and consider reaching out to your team members. This proactive approach sends a powerful message: you're open to improving, and their insights matter to you. For instance, try asking, *What's one thing I could have done differently on that project?* or *How did my approach impact the team?* Regularly gathering these insights helps you understand how your actions are perceived, allowing you to fine-tune your approach and build deeper connections within your team.

Use Feedback to Create Actionable Steps for Improvement: Receiving feedback is only the first part. You're going to need to transform it into tangible actions to get real growth. Once you have constructive insights, break them down into clear, manageable steps you can act on. For example, if you receive feedback about improving your presentation skills, make it an actionable goal: practice presenting to a mentor, take a public speaking course, or review each presentation afterward to identify areas of improvement. These incremental steps don't have to be monumental to make an impact. Each is a small win that adds up over time. Setting actionable steps based on feedback helps you transform criticism into meaningful growth.

By embracing feedback, you cultivate resilience, adaptability, and a deeper commitment to your development. Leaders who actively seek out and act on feedback send a message that growth is never complete and that there's always room to improve.

Maria was an executive assistant who became a good friend of mine. She was a brilliant problem-solver and always ready to tackle challenges to support her senior leadership team. However, each time her manager called her in for feedback, Maria told me that she felt anxious. She feared that even minor critiques could put her job at risk.

In her mind, feedback highlighted her shortcomings, and she worried that any perceived missteps might lead to consequences she couldn't control. This fear held her back from fully engaging in feedback sessions, sometimes making her defensive or overly cautious, as she struggled to see feedback as anything other than a threat.

Recognizing her anxiety, Maria's manager took steps to create an environment of psychological safety. During each feedback session, her manager emphasized that feedback was meant to support Maria's professional growth and help her expand her already impressive skill set rather than critique her abilities or put her job security at risk.

Gradually, Maria began to see that feedback could be an opportunity for growth rather than a judgment on her performance. Her manager's supportive approach created a space where Maria felt comfortable asking clarifying questions and acknowledging areas where she could improve. This shift allowed her to reframe feedback to gain insights and deepen her understanding of her role.

As Maria grew more comfortable receiving feedback, she took a more proactive approach, regularly seeking input from her manager and colleagues. She began to view each conversation as an opportunity to expand her skills and anticipate the evolving needs of the executives she supported. This mindset shift eased her anxiety and empowered her to make improvements confidently and easily adapt her strategies.

Cultivate the Habit of Reflection

Reflection is one of the most effective tools for deepening learning and fostering growth. In the rush to meet deadlines, juggle responsibilities, and push forward, it's tempting to think there's no time to pause. But without reflection, you're running on autopilot, missing the chance to learn from your experiences and refine your approach.

Taking even a small amount of time to reflect can unlock insights that drive performance, build resilience, and deepen your sense of purpose. And when you regularly reflect on your work, you not only perform better but also develop a stronger capacity to navigate challenges.[7]

Reflection gives you the space to connect the dots, to understand not just *what* happened but *why* it happened and *how* you can improve. It's a habit that transforms experiences into lessons and lessons into growth.

To make reflection a regular part of your routine, start small but be intentional.

Schedule a Weekly Reflection Session: Block out time in your calendar, even if it's just 20 minutes at the end of the week. Treat this as a sacred appointment with yourself. During this time, ask questions like: *What did I accomplish this week? What challenges did I face, and how did I handle them? What can I do differently moving forward?* Remember that this isn't about perfection. It's about learning and recalibrating. The act of slowing down to assess your week helps you approach the future with greater clarity and intention.

Turn Insights into Actionable Adjustments: Reflection is most powerful when it leads to change. Take the lessons you uncover and transform them into specific, actionable steps. For example, if you notice that a lack of preparation caused stress during a presentation, commit to a new habit of allocating prep time in your calendar. If you struggle with a communication issue, brainstorm how you can address it more effectively next time.

Rewire Your Brain by Celebrating Small Wins

Our brains are wired for survival, not happiness. Neuropsychologist Dr. Rick Hanson[8] explains that the brain's natural "negativity bias" makes us hyperaware of setbacks, mistakes, and dangers. This instinct, while essential for our ancestors avoiding predators, often keeps us stuck in a loop of self-criticism and doubt. We focus on what went wrong and downplay what went right, leaving little room to recognize progress or celebrate achievements.

But you can retrain your brain. By intentionally celebrating small wins, you can counteract this negativity bias and create new mental pathways rooted in positivity and resilience. This practice shifts your focus from what's lacking, to what you're building, encouraging a mindset of growth and possibility. Celebrating small wins isn't just a feel-good activity. It's a powerful way to reframe how you see challenges and progress.

Here's how to begin rewiring your brain for positivity:

Acknowledge Daily Accomplishments: In the rush of daily life, it's easy to overlook the small victories that mark your progress. Take a moment each day to recognize something you achieved, no matter how minor it seems. Maybe you pushed through a challenging task, learned something new, or simply showed up for a tough conversation. By pausing to acknowledge these moments, you reinforce your progress and send a message to your brain: *This matters.*

Dr. Hanson suggests that intentionally "taking in the good" helps positive experiences sink into your mental framework.[9] The key is to linger on these moments for a few seconds longer than usual. Feel the accomplishment, no matter how small, and allow yourself to absorb its significance. Over time, this practice helps reshape your thinking, making it easier to see the good in every day.

Reflect on How Far You've Come: When you're caught in the grind, it's easy to lose sight of your growth. Progress can feel slow or even invisible. In those moments, pause to reflect on your journey. Think about where you started, the obstacles you've faced, and the lessons you've learned along the way.

By looking back with intention, you'll start to see patterns of resilience and growth. Challenges that once felt insurmountable now serve as evidence of your perseverance. This reflection reinforces the belief that consistent effort leads to meaningful progress. It reminds you that every small step you take is part of a bigger story of transformation.

Activity 11 Stacking Small Wins for Growth

Step 1: Choose Three Areas to Improve

Select three areas where you'd like to grow, such as:

- **Skill Development** (e.g., learning something new).
- **Feedback Integration** (e.g., acting on feedback).
- **Reflection** (e.g., weekly check-ins with yourself).

Step 2: Set One Small Action for Each

Define a small, easy step for each area. For example:

- Spend ten minutes a day on learning a new skill.
- Ask for feedback on one project each week.
- Reflect on a lesson learned at the end of your week.

Step 3: Track Your Wins

Keep a simple log each week. Write down:

- The action you took.
- One thing you learned or achieved.

Step 4: Review Monthly

At the end of each month, review your progress. Ask:

- What's improved?
- What steps made the biggest difference?

This simple habit of stacking wins will help you stay focused, motivated, and growth-oriented.

Embracing Setbacks as Opportunities for Growth

Adopting a growth mindset doesn't mean setbacks will disappear. Setbacks are inevitable on any path toward meaningful progress. The difference lies in how you respond when they arise. High performers with a growth mindset view these moments not as roadblocks but as stepping stones, using each challenge to refine their approach and build resilience. When setbacks arise, they ask themselves:

What Can I Learn from This? Instead of internalizing the setback as a personal failure, they focus on extracting lessons to inform their next steps.

How Can I Adapt My Approach? Setbacks often signal the need for a pivot or a new strategy. Rather than giving up, those with a growth mindset seek ways to evolve and improve.

Who Can I Seek Guidance from to Overcome This Challenge? Growth-minded individuals recognize the value of reaching out to mentors, colleagues, or experts to gain fresh insights and support.

The idea of "learning from mistakes" is not a new concept and is often referred to as **failing forward**[10] or **failing fast.**[11] And people who see setbacks as learning moments rather than personal failures are more likely to adapt, persist, and ultimately succeed.

Turning setbacks into growth opportunities requires a shift in perspective and a willingness to see beyond immediate disappointment. Here's how to begin embracing setbacks in a way that fuels growth:

Reframe Failure as Feedback

In a fixed mindset, failure is a verdict. But in a growth mindset, failure is simply feedback or guidance on where to adapt, improve, and move forward. Matt Spielman[12] explores this concept in his book on purposeful living, encouraging us to see setbacks as opportunities to realign with what truly matters. Learning to reframe failure in this way keeps you focused on growth, not limitations, and drives you toward lasting fulfillment.

I'll never forget a project early in my career that taught me the value of setbacks as opportunities for learning. I was responsible for a high-stakes initiative to reduce workplace incidents. I'd poured myself into the project, gathering data, training staff, and even bringing in expensive consultants to support the work.

Despite all the preparation, the initial rollout didn't yield the results I expected. Incident rates barely shifted, and I felt like I'd failed. I was disheartened, wondering if I'd miscalculated or overlooked something critical. But as tempting as it was to let the outcome reinforce my self-doubt, I decided to approach it differently.

I asked myself three questions to turn this failure into feedback:

What Went Wrong? I took an honest, objective look at what I could have done differently. Rather than seeing the project as a failure, I looked at specific areas, such as employee engagement during training, where I hadn't gained the buy-in I'd hoped for.

What Did I Learn? Reflecting on the experience, I realized I needed more time involving team leaders at an earlier stage. Their insights could have helped me shape the project to fit the organization's unique needs better.

What's My Next Step? Armed with these insights, I refined my approach for future initiatives. Instead of pushing forward with my assumptions, I prioritized collaboration with on-the-ground staff.

This experience transformed the way I approached setbacks. By viewing each challenge as feedback, I was able to focus on how each step (success or setback) could shape my next move.

Develop Resilience through Optimism

Building resilience is tied to the power of optimism. Positive psychology research shows that optimistic individuals recover more quickly and fully from setbacks. But optimism isn't about denying challenges or pretending that everything is easy. This form of resilience comes from knowing that, even in difficult times, you have the strength, resources, and support to find a path forward.

To cultivate resilience through optimism, try these practices:

Embrace Realistic Optimism: This isn't about blind positivity but about facing difficulties with confidence in your ability to work through them. Realistic optimism means acknowledging the obstacles without letting them overshadow your potential to find solutions. When setbacks arise, give yourself a moment to recognize and process any fear or doubt. Then, focus on actionable steps. Ask yourself, *What's within my control?* and *What small step can I take today?* Each small, forward-focused action builds resilience by reinforcing your belief in your capacity to adapt and grow.

Build a Resilient Support Network: Surround yourself with people who not only encourage you but also challenge you to see your strengths and potential. Supportive people remind us of our resilience, even when we can't see it ourselves. Consider who in your circle truly lifts you up, offers honest advice, and helps you refocus on what matters. Reach out to those individuals when you need perspective or a reminder of your strengths. Over time, a strong support network nurtures your resilience and adds optimism that keeps you moving forward.

Reframe Setbacks as Temporary, Not Permanent: Resilient optimism comes from seeing setbacks as short-term challenges rather than permanent roadblocks. When difficulties arise, remind yourself that they're part of the journey, not the end of it. By reframing setbacks this way, you train your mind to see adversity as a phase rather than a defining limit on your future. This mindset shift creates room for hope and possibility, making it easier to take risks, face challenges, and persevere through even the most demanding situations.

Seek Support and Mentorship

Growth is rarely a solo journey, and the most resilient leaders understand the value of learning from others. Social learning theory, developed by psychologist Albert Bandura,[13] emphasizes that much of our growth comes from observing, interacting, and collaborating with others. When we engage with people who have faced similar challenges, we gain new perspectives, skills, and insights that broaden our approach and deepen our resilience. Seeking support and mentorship is not just a tool for growth but a foundation for a mindset that sees every interaction as an opportunity to learn.

To make the most of mentorship and social learning, consider these approaches:

Seek Guidance from a Mentor: A mentor is more than a guide. They have navigated the challenges you may be facing and can provide valuable insights and encouragement. Don't hesitate to reach out to someone who inspires you. Whether you need specific advice or a broader perspective, a mentor can offer feedback and help you see the bigger picture, making challenges seem more manageable.

Collaborate with Peers Who Have Overcome Similar Challenges: Learning from peers can be equally powerful. Those who recently faced similar obstacles can share fresh insights, practical advice, and realistic strategies. Collaborating with others fosters a sense of camaraderie and creates a supportive environment where everyone's experiences contribute to growth. These peer-to-peer connections often lead to new ideas and a more balanced perspective on problem-solving.

Leverage Your Professional Network for Ideas and Support: Your network is valuable. Reach out and let others know about the challenges you're tackling. Not only can they offer different viewpoints, but they may also connect you to resources or individuals you hadn't considered. A quick check-in with a colleague can spark ideas or provide clarity that helps you move forward. Networks can serve as a wellspring of inspiration and reassurance, reminding you that you don't have to navigate growth alone.

Activity 12 Turning Setbacks into Springboards for Growth

This activity helps you reframe setbacks as valuable opportunities to learn, adapt, and grow.

Step 1: Reflect on a Recent Setback

Think of a recent challenge or setback, whether it was a missed goal, a challenging project, or unexpected feedback. Write down a brief description of what happened, focusing on the specifics without assigning blame to yourself or others.

Step 2: Ask Three Key Questions

Use these questions to dig into the experience and extract valuable insights: **What can I learn from this?, How can I adapt my approach?, Who can I seek guidance from?**

Step 3: Outline One Next Step

Create a simple action step based on your answers to apply what you've learned. This step could be a specific change in your approach, a conversation you plan to have, or a skill you want to strengthen.

Step 4: Check Your Perspective

To build resilience through optimism, reframe the setback as a temporary hurdle rather than a permanent limitation. Write a sentence affirming your ability to overcome similar challenges in the future.

By completing this activity regularly, you'll develop a habit of viewing setbacks as building blocks that guide you forward, strengthening your resilience and growth mindset over time.

Leading with a Growth Mindset

Leading with a growth mindset goes beyond personal career advancement. It fundamentally elevates how you empower and connect with others. When you, as a leader, demonstrate curiosity, openness, and resilience in the face of challenges, you're laying the foundation for a culture that values learning over perfection.

Dr. Daniel Goleman,[14] a pioneer in emotional intelligence, notes that growth-oriented leaders are uniquely positioned to inspire their teams to embrace challenges, think creatively, and redefine what's possible. These types of leaders encourage team members to see challenges as opportunities, not obstacles. In doing so, they nurture an environment of psychological safety, where individuals feel safe to experiment, share unconventional ideas, and learn from their mistakes.

Creating a growth-minded culture begins with recognizing and valuing the journey over the destination. As a growth-oriented leader, you celebrate the process as much as the outcome.

You openly acknowledge that setbacks are part of learning, encouraging your team to take calculated risks. When team members feel free to try new approaches without fearing judgment, they're more likely to innovate and push boundaries, knowing that you're interested in their insights, not just the result. This freedom to explore helps individuals step into their potential, fueling not only their growth but also the team's overall success.

A crucial element of leading with a growth mindset is encouraging **experimentation**. Freedom to experiment fuels a cycle of innovation as team members learn from each attempt, refining their ideas and discovering new possibilities.

A leader with a growth mindset knows the importance of modeling **vulnerability**. Showing that you don't have all the answers and are willing to learn from others demonstrates authenticity and openness, which creates trust. This kind of honesty builds a culture where growth is a shared journey, and no one is afraid to say, "I don't know, but I'm willing to find out." The result is a more cohesive team that tackles challenges collaboratively, knowing they can rely on each other for support and insights.

A growth-minded leader recognizes the **unique strengths** each team member brings and actively cultivates them. You view talent development as a mission to help each person realize their potential. Leaders with a growth mindset invest time in understanding the aspirations, skills, and challenges of their team members, using these insights to create growth opportunities.

Lastly, growth-minded leaders embrace challenges and change as **catalysts for progress**. When your team encounters obstacles, you frame them as valuable learning experiences rather than setbacks. In these moments, your mindset sets the tone: by focusing on what can be gained from each challenge, you encourage resilience and adaptability. Over time, this approach helps your team view obstacles as temporary hurdles, not dead-ends, making them more capable of handling change and uncertainty.

In leading with a growth mindset, you're equipping your team with the skills, confidence, and resilience to meet future challenges. You create an environment where curiosity, adaptability, and optimism are foundational, allowing you and your team to navigate the complexities of today's dynamic work environment with purpose and strength. Through fostering a culture of growth, you leave a legacy of empowerment and possibility, transforming your team and organization from the inside out.

Encourage Experimentation

Research reveals a powerful link between psychological safety, innovation, and organizational success.[15] Companies that actively foster a culture of psychological safety and encourage experimentation significantly outperform their competitors in growth, resilience, and adaptability.[16]

When leaders embrace experimentation, they're not only opening the door to creative problem-solving but also building a workplace where team members feel empowered to take risks without fear of criticism or failure.

Leaders who promote experimentation create an environment where team members can test new ideas, explore unconventional approaches, and learn from setbacks with confidence. They understand that innovation rarely follows a straight path and that growth requires trial and error. In these environments, failure isn't seen as a setback but as an opportunity for valuable learning.

Model Vulnerability

As we explored earlier with Dr. Brené Brown's research on vulnerability, leaders who openly acknowledge that they don't have all the answers can build deep trust and genuine respect within their teams. Vulnerability in leadership isn't a weakness but is a powerful way to connect with others on a human level. When leaders are willing to admit their uncertainties and growth areas, they create an atmosphere where team members feel safe to take risks, ask questions, and embrace challenges without fear of judgment.

Modeling vulnerability means embracing the idea that growth and learning (not perfection) are the ultimate goals. By sharing your own experiences with failure, whether it's a project that fell apart or moments of self-doubt, you allow your team to see that setbacks are simply steps toward improvement, not personal failures. To effectively model vulnerability, try these actions:

Share Your Challenges and Ask for Input: Start by opening up about something specific you're working on and invite feedback. For example, say,

I've been working on communicating more clearly in meetings. How could I do this better? This not only shows humility but also encourages your team to be honest about their growth areas.

Acknowledge Mistakes and What You're Learning: When you make a misstep, discuss it openly with the team. For example, *I realized I could have handled that project update differently. Here's what I'm learning from this experience. What would you have done in that situation?*

Express Uncertainty in a Productive Way: In challenging situations, say something like, *I don't have all the answers here, but I'd like us to figure it out together.* This shows that you value collaborative problem-solving and aren't afraid of the unknown. It also models that it's okay not to know everything as long as you're committed to finding solutions.

Invite Others to Share Their Own Learning Experiences: Create a safe space in team meetings where you ask, *What's one thing you tried recently that didn't go as expected, and what did you learn?* Sharing these stories creates a culture of openness and growth, showing everyone has room to develop.

Encouraging your team to take on projects that challenge their skills, even if they feel unsure about the outcome, also fosters vulnerability. Emphasize that uncertainty is a natural part of growth and that progress, not perfection, is the true mark of success. Leading in this way, you help shift your team's focus from flawless execution to the courage to learn, experiment, and build resilience.

Focus on Developing Your Team

Leaders with a growth mindset understand that their success is measured by the growth of their teams.[17] Investing in your team's development creates a culture of engagement, trust, and improvement across the entire organization. And employees who feel supported in their growth and development demonstrate higher engagement, productivity, and loyalty.[18]

Here are some impactful ways to actively support your team's development:

Encourage Ongoing Skill Building: Motivate team members to expand their abilities by offering access to workshops, online courses, or time for self-directed learning. Emphasize that skill development is part of everyone's role and is valued at every level. Ask your team, *What's one area you're interested in exploring further, and how can I support you?* By actively fostering skill building, you empower employees to take charge of their growth.

Deliver Constructive Feedback with a Focus on Growth: Feedback is one of the most powerful tools for development when it's delivered thoughtfully. Frame feedback as an opportunity to strengthen skills and address challenges. Instead of pointing out areas for improvement, offer suggestions on how they might try different approaches in the future and ask, *What would you like to adjust next time, and how can I support that?*

Celebrate Small Wins and Reflect on Progress: Building confidence and resilience comes not only from significant achievements but also from small, steady wins. Regularly acknowledge and celebrate the progress your team makes, even in small steps. After a challenging project, encourage reflection by asking, *What went well, and what did you learn?* Celebrating these incremental successes helps team members see their development in real terms, boosting both engagement and motivation.

Create a Development Plan for Each Team Member: Take time to understand each person's aspirations, strengths, and areas for improvement. Sit down with each team member to develop a personalized growth plan, setting short-term and long-term goals. This might involve identifying new skills to build, future roles to work toward, or specific challenges to tackle. Revisiting these plans regularly signals their progress is a priority, showing that you're invested in their journey and success.

By focusing on developing your team, you cultivate an environment where growth is a shared goal. When team members feel valued and supported in their growth, they're more likely to invest fully in their roles, contribute meaningfully, and support one another. Leaders who prioritize development foster a culture where everyone is encouraged to reach their potential, creating a foundation of trust, mutual respect, and a collective drive toward excellence.

Activity 13 Reflect, Reset, Repeat: Growth in Action

Encourage your team to take a few minutes each week to reflect on a challenge or project they've tackled recently. Ask them to identify:

1 *One lesson learned from the experience.*
2 *One small success* that moved them closer to their goal, even if the result wasn't perfect.
3 *One idea* for how they might approach a similar challenge differently next time.

Encourage sharing these reflections in a team meeting to foster a culture of learning, resilience, and openness, allowing everyone to see challenges as opportunities to grow.

Turning Mindset into Momentum

Adopting a growth mindset equips you with resilience, adaptability, and the innovative edge needed for the future. In fast-evolving industries, where new challenges and opportunities constantly arise, a growth mindset is essential.

The World Economic Forum's *Future of Jobs Report*[19] highlights that skills like problem-solving, critical thinking, and adaptability are among the most desired by employers. A growth mindset strengthens these abilities and can transform the way you approach both personal and professional growth.

To make this mindset your fuel, here's a roadmap for turning insights into action:

Conduct a Growth Audit: Identify the areas where you feel stuck and ask, *Where can I grow?* Reflect on your experiences and notice patterns where you can push past your comfort zone.

Set Learning Goals: Move beyond performance targets and set goals centered on learning and exploration. Whether mastering a new skill or tackling a challenging project, these goals will keep you focused on growth rather than outcomes.

Track Your Progress: Keep a growth journal to capture your challenges, breakthroughs, and reflections.

Build a Support Network: Surround yourself with mentors, peers, and colleagues who support your journey. A strong network encourages growth by providing new perspectives and constructive feedback.

Embrace Setbacks as Lessons: Shift your perspective to view setbacks as essential parts of growth. When things don't go as planned, use it as a chance to analyze, learn, and improve.

Each step on this journey reinforces your commitment to growth and your ability to turn challenges into opportunities. In time, this mindset will become second nature, fueling not only your professional journey but your personal one as well. By making growth a steady priority, you're creating a foundation that can support and elevate every future ambition.

Unlocking Possibility

Embracing a growth mindset helps you choose resilience, adaptability, and the courage to see every challenge as an opportunity. You're no longer bound by past limitations or perfectionism. Instead, you're embracing a mindset that values learning, evolution, and pushing the boundaries of what feels familiar.

In this chapter, we've explored how a growth mindset can ignite lasting change, not only within yourself but also in those you lead. You've seen how practices like conducting a growth audit, setting learning goals, welcoming feedback, and creating psychological safety can turn small steps into powerful momentum. Each effort, no matter how subtle, fortifies your foundation and empowers you to inspire progress in yourself and those around you. By embracing setbacks as lessons and celebrating even the tiniest wins, you're building a mindset that fuels personal and collective growth.

But stepping out of the comfort zone is just the start. True transformation comes when you use this mindset to build a distinct, impactful presence. Now, it's time to channel that momentum toward uncovering your unique strengths. Growth readies you to adapt, but knowing and articulating your unique value is what will set you apart. In the next chapter, we'll explore how to design your **unique value proposition** (**UVP**), which is the cornerstone of what makes you stand out in your field.

Notes

1 Dweck, C. S. 2006. *Mindset: The New Psychology of Success*. Ballantine Books.
2 Moser, J. S., H. S. Schroder, C. Heeter, T. P. Moran, and Y. H. Lee. 2011. "Mind Your Errors: Evidence for a Neural Mechanism Linking Growth Mindset to Adaptive Post-Error Adjustments." *Psychological Science* 22(12): 1484–1489. https://doi.org/10.1177/0956797611419520.
3 Brown, B. 2018. *Dare to Lead: Brave Work. Tough Conversations. Whole Hearts*. Random House.
4 Amazon. n.d. "Leadership Principles." *About Amazon*. Accessed 12 February 2024. https://www.aboutamazon.com/about-us/leadership-principles.
5 Moser, J. S., H. S. Schroder, C. Heeter, T. P. Moran, and Y. H. Lee. 2011. "Mind Your Errors: Evidence for a Neural Mechanism Linking Growth Mindset to Adaptive Posterror Adjustments." *Psychological Science* 22(12): 1484–1489. https://doi.org/10.1177/0956797611419520.
6 Stone, D., and S. Heen. 2015. *Thanks for the Feedback: The Science and Art of Receiving Feedback Well*. Penguin Books.
7 Di Stefano, G., G. Pisano, and B. R. Staats. 2015. Learning by Thinking: How Reflection Can Spur Progress Along the Learning Curve. Harvard Business School NOM Unit Working Paper No. 14-093, Kenan Institute of Private Enterprise Research Paper No. 2414478. http://dx.doi.org/10.2139/ssrn.2414478.
8 Hanson, R. 2013. *Hardwiring Happiness: The New Brain Science of Contentment, Calm, and Confidence*. Harmony.
9 Hanson, R., and F. Hanson. 2018. *Resilient: How to Grow an Unshakable Core of Calm, Strength, and Happiness*. Harmony.
10 Maxwell, J. C. 2007. *Failing Forward: Turning Mistakes into Stepping Stones for Success*. Thomas Nelson.
11 Tulsidas, L. 2024. *Failing Fast?: The Ten Secrets to Succeed Faster*. Forbes Books.
12 Spielman, M. 2022. *Inflection Points: How to Work and Live with Purpose*. Wiley.
13 Bandura, A. 1976. *Social Learning Theory*. Prentice-Hall.

14 Goleman, D. 2005. *Emotional Intelligence: Why It Can Matter More Than IQ*. Bantam Books.
15 Edmondson, A. C. 2019. *The Fearless Organization: Creating Psychological Safety in the Workplace for Learning, Innovation, and Growth*. Wiley.
16 Thomke, S. H. 2020. *Experimentation Works: The Surprising Power of Business Experiments*. Harvard Business Review Press.
17 McKinsey & Company. 2021. "Reimagining People Development to Overcome Talent Challenges." *McKinsey & Company*. https://www.mckinsey.com/capabilities/people-and-organizational-performance/our-insights/reimagining-people-development-to-overcome-talent-challenges.
18 Harvard Business Review. 2022. "Why Upskilling Your Workforce Is Essential in Today's Economy." *Harvard Business Review*. https://www.hbs.edu/managing-the-future-of-work/podcast/Pages/default.aspx?Topic=Reskilling+and+Upskilling.
19 World Economic Forum. 2023. *The Future of Jobs Report 2023*. World Economic Forum. https://www.weforum.org/publications/the-future-of-jobs-report-2023/.

Chapter 3

What Only You Can Bring

"Have you ever wondered if your work truly matters – if *you* truly matter?"

It's a question that sneaks up on you in quiet moments, often when you least expect it. For years, I poured myself into my work. I chased promotions, hit milestones, and followed the playbook for building a successful career in corporate America. And yet, beneath the surface of achievement, there was a whisper I couldn't ignore:

What makes me different?

If I stripped away the job titles and awards, what story did I want my career to tell to others and, most importantly, to myself?

I didn't want to be just another name in a sea of professionals, defined by bullet points on a résumé. I wanted to feel irreplaceable. Not because I worked harder than anyone else but because the impact I made would be uniquely mine. I wanted to know that my work wasn't just filling a role but creating a legacy that only I could leave behind.

The ache for meaning in your work isn't just a passing thought.

It's an invitation to uncover your *unique value proposition (UVP), or* what you alone bring to the table.

Your UVP isn't just about defining your career. It's about finding alignment between who you are, what you do, and the difference you make. And while it sounds simple, uncovering it isn't easy. It takes facing those difficult questions:

Who am I without the job titles?

What impact do I want to leave behind?

What's the story I want my career to tell, not just to others, but to myself?

This is about peeling back the layers, beyond the accolades and credentials, to find the qualities that are uniquely yours. Think of your UVP as a mirror to show yourself, in the clearest terms, why you do what you do and why that matters.

DOI: 10.4324/9781003627265-4

In this chapter, you'll learn how to craft a UVP that's not a slogan but a statement of purpose that carries the weight of your experiences, values, and vision for the future.

By the end, you'll have a UVP that feels like an extension of yourself. A purpose that grounds you and reminds you that you are here to do something only *you* can do. Standing out today isn't about doing more. It's about stripping away the unnecessary to reveal what's unmistakably you.

Finding the Story Only You Can Tell

In a world full of noise, it's easy to blend in. To follow the crowd and adopt the habits, language, and style that others have paved before us.

I know how to do this painfully well. As an immigrant to the United States who, after more than 20 years of living here, still has my Australian accent. As someone who wants to fit in, yet gets asked *Where are you from?* and my answer of "Seattle" leaves them puzzled.

An understanding that I have had to mask who I really am, in order to build a successful career. For years, I would shut down any questions about my children, even if they were well meaning. I was afraid that being a mother would be the reason that I didn't get the career break or the big opportunity.

I dressed in the corporate uniform. Sometimes it was suits and high heels. Other times, it was jeans and sneakers. All to fit in. To conform with the rubric of how to be successful.

But here's something I've realized. It was *exactly those things* – the funny accent, the quirky take on life, having three children and three dogs (can't forget the dogs, can we?) – that made me stand out. And sure, while some of my traits and quirks weren't everyone's cup of tea, they were mine.

Because if you want to be truly unforgettable, blending in won't get you there. The real power of differentiation comes from daring to stand apart in a way that feels deeply, authentically you.

Think about people that made an impression *on you. Why do you still remember them, maybe decades later?*

I remember once when I was headhunted by a wise executive recruiter for a senior global role. During one of the first conversations, I recited details from my resume, my achievements, my knowledge, and skills. The recruiter stopped me mid-sentence. "Megan, you're a change agent. You're a transformational leader."

Those few words helped me see what I was and wasn't. I was not a technical expert but a leader who brought strategy, process, and people together to drive change in complex, challenging situations.

Can you see the shift? What about you? What's your story?

You, too, have your own story. Let's use the Story Method in Activity 14, to craft your UVP.

Activity 14 Craft Your UVP with the Story Method

Your story is the key to crafting a UVP that feels authentic and meaningful. Use this simple exercise to uncover the moments that define your unique value.

1 **Reflect on Defining Moments**
Identify three key moments in your career when:

- You overcame a challenge.
- You made a significant impact.
- You experienced a shift that shaped how you work.

For each moment, ask yourself:

- **Who** benefited from your work?
- **What** was the tangible result or outcome?
- **Why** did it matter to you personally?

2 **Craft Your UVP**
Combine your reflections into a concise statement using this formula:
"I help [who] achieve [what] by leveraging my [core strength/approach], driven by my commitment to [why]."
Example: "I help first-time leaders grow into confident decision-makers by leveraging lessons from my career pivots, driven by my passion for empowering others to thrive in uncertainty."

3 **Refine and Reflect**

- Read your UVP aloud. Does it feel authentic? Does it reflect what matters most to you?
- Adjust as needed to ensure it captures not just your skills but your deeper purpose.

Letting Your Story Shine

Every interaction you have leaves an impression, whether in a meeting, a question on Slack, or a casual conversation. People will notice your accomplishments, skills, and results, but they rarely take the time to uncover the deep layers of what makes you unique. *Why do you approach problems the way you do? What motivates you? What sets you apart in a way that only you can bring to the table?*

These are questions that move you from being merely noticed to being unforgettable. This is where differentiation begins. Not by blending in, but by embracing the qualities that make you stand out.

You may have heard of the **Similarity Attraction Effect**, which explains why we naturally connect with people who share something in common with us. But remember, shared values, experiences, or perspectives build rapport, but they don't make you memorable. Differentiation happens when you go deeper, daring to show what's distinct about you.

Think about it this way.

The similarity attraction effect might open the door, but it's your story that keeps someone's attention. The special stories, the hard-won lessons, and the unique way you see the world create a lasting connection. Letting your story shine requires you to lean into what sets you apart and articulate it in a way that is authentic and relevant to the challenges and needs of those you aim to serve.

Dr. Adam Grant, professor at Wharton and author of *Originals*,[1] teaches us that those who succeed are those willing to stand by their unique qualities, even when it means stepping away from the status quo. Differentiation demands **courage** (we'll talk more about courage in Chapter 4). It asks you to step out of the crowd and declare, *This is who I am, and this is why it matters.*

By connecting through shared experiences while daring to reveal your true self, you create a powerful balance of relatability and individuality. You're no longer just another face in the room. You're a voice and presence that others remember and respect.

So, what does this mean for your **unique value proposition**?

It means crafting a UVP that doesn't rely on cliches or generalities but draws from the core of who you are. After all, it's not about reinventing yourself but peeling back the layers to reveal your authentic story.

As we continue, think about this:

What's the story only you can tell? How can it set you apart in a way that feels true to you?

The answers to these questions hold the key to creating a UVP that is a reflection of your purpose, your passion, and your potential to leave a lasting legacy.

And remember, your identity can change over time. We are ever-evolving human beings. If you're feeling a bit stuck, go back to Activity 6. I've found that whenever I feel confused or unsure, going back to my values is a good starting point to think about where to start my story.

Your UVP Superpower: Own It, Show It

Think of your UVP as something that makes your work meaningful, irreplaceable, and uniquely yours. When done well, your UVP becomes a

A strong UVP is built on three essential pillars:

1. **Core Strengths and Skills:** What are you exceptionally good at? Which skills or qualities set you apart?
2. **Industry or Organizational Needs:** What are the most pressing challenges in your industry or organization, and how does your expertise align with those needs?
3. **Differentiation:** What is the unique value only you bring? Why should others choose you above anyone else?

Figure 3.1 The Three Pillars of an Impactful UVP.

powerful statement that resonates on a personal level and tells others not just what you do but why you're the only one who can do it in the way you do.

Imagine this. You're standing in front of a room full of people, and they're waiting to hear *your* story. Not your job title, not your qualifications, but *your story*. This is the heart of your UVP.

But crafting a UVP isn't a matter of gathering a few bullet points. You're going to need to amplify the qualities that make you unforgettable.

Look at Figure 3.1, for a breakdown of the elements of a UVP that captures your strengths, meets a pressing need, and sets you apart as the obvious choice.

Let's work through each of these pillars, looking at not just the *what* but the *why* and *how* behind each element.

Pillar 1: Identifying Your Core Strengths and Skills: What Lights You Up?

Self-awareness is at the core of a compelling UVP. In positive psychology, the concept of *strength-based leadership*, developed by Dr. Martin Seligman[2] and Dr. Donald Clifton,[3] emphasizes that leaders who lead with their strengths experience higher engagement and success. Rather than improving weaknesses, strength-based leadership is about doubling down on what you're naturally good at.

So, remember those moments in your career when you felt genuinely proud of your work. *What were you doing? Why did it feel so meaningful?* These moments are often clues pointing to your core strengths.

Reflect on this: you might have a technically impressive skill, but if it doesn't bring you energy or joy, it won't become part of a UVP that feels authentic. When identifying your strengths, go beyond surface-level abilities. Look for the strengths connected to your values and purpose, the things you would still be doing even if no one was watching. These are the skills that make you come alive, give meaning to your work, and shape your professional identity.

Practical Steps to Uncover Your Core Strengths and Skills

Reflect on Past Successes: What were the moments in your career that brought a deep sense of accomplishment? Think about not just *what* you achieved, but *how* you achieved it. What personal strengths came into play?

Seek Out External Perspectives: Sometimes, others see strengths in us that we take for granted. Ask trusted colleagues, mentors, or friends what they see as your standout qualities.

Use Strengths Assessments: Tools like StrengthsFinder[4] or the VIA Character Strengths Survey[5] can provide insights into your natural strengths, helping you understand your unique blend of capabilities.

Pillar 2: Understanding Industry or Organizational Needs: Where You Meet the Moment

The best UVPs aren't just about *you* but about how your unique skills meet a real, urgent need. This alignment creates relevance, positioning you as the answer to a specific question your industry or organization is already asking.

Funnily enough, it's also what helps you secure a new job, attract your ideal client, or seize the right opportunity. You're solving their problem. Sometimes even one they don't realize they have yet.

Years ago, I learned the importance of *making things easier for* others. Whether it was helping my students grasp new concepts when I was an academic, or simply organizing a meeting, simplifying processes opened doors. The same principles apply here: understanding the key issues shaping your field allows you to address the challenges others face.

Is it rapid technological change?

A shift in consumer expectations?

Increased emphasis on sustainability?

Whatever the trend, understanding these needs allows you to shape a UVP that goes beyond developing skills and positions you as a strategic thinker who sees the bigger picture and actively contributes to it.

The most valuable leaders are those who can look around corners, connect dots, and execute (or build a rockstar team that can). Being the person who brings meaningful solutions to the table transforms you from competent to indispensable. This requires curiosity, foresight, and a willingness to step back and see the bigger picture.

For example, consider someone in supply chain management during a time of global disruption. It's not enough to simply optimize processes.

A great leader in this space might identify new technologies to improve forecasting, propose strategies for diversifying suppliers, or build cross-functional collaboration to manage risk. By tackling the broader issues shaping their field, they elevate their role from operational to strategic.

You're not just answering the question, *Why you?* You're leaving them thinking, *How could we not move forward without you?*

As we continue, you'll learn how to weave your unique qualities, personal story, and understanding of industry needs into a UVP that feels authentic and powerfully relevant. Because relevance transforms your strengths into impact, and impact creates lasting value.

Here are three practical steps to understand industry or organizational needs.

1 **Research Industry Trends: Tune in to the Shifts**

To know where you fit, you need to know what's changing. Follow the news, attend conferences, read industry reports, and pay attention to the conversations happening around you. *Are there recurring themes? Common challenges?*

For instance, are leaders in your industry talking about digital transformation and the struggle to keep up with rapid technological advances? Or is there a growing call for transparency and ethics in business practices? These themes are often signposts pointing to areas where you can have an impact.

2 **Understand Your Organization's Goals: Connect on a Personal Level**

Every organization has its unique set of strategic goals and values that shape priorities, decision-making, and, ultimately, what success looks like. By aligning your UVP with these goals, you demonstrate that you're not just a contributor but invested in the mission.

Take time to understand these goals.

Is your organization focused on rapid innovation? Are they striving to enhance customer experience, reduce their environmental impact, or become a leader in diversity, equity, and inclusion?

This is where your UVP takes on new meaning. When you tailor your UVP to reflect your strengths and how those strengths advance your organization's goals, you position yourself as an essential part of the team. For example, if you're part of a sustainability-focused company, aligning your UVP around creating long-term, ethical solutions shows that you're not just fulfilling a role, you're building a future alongside them.

3 **Study Your Worthy Rivals: Find Your Place in the Landscape**

Simon Sinek[6] explores the concept of worthy rivals in his book, *The Infinite Game*. When I was at Netflix, I was lucky enough to attend a weeklong leadership seminar where we studied this concept. My take is that worthy rivals are worthy of comparison but they don't need to be your competitors. It's a simple yet distinct nuance and helps you to stay creatively minded by not focusing on competition, about staying true to yourself, but learning from others.

Your worthy rivals can be one of your greatest teachers. Analyzing others in similar roles or fields reveals what strengths and approaches are already valued and where there might be room for you to stand out. Study their profiles, observe how they position themselves, and note the language they use to describe their expertise.

Finally, identifying gaps in the market can be a powerful way to sharpen your UVP. If most communications specialists, for example, focus on technical skills, you might emphasize your ability to convey warmth, build emotional connection, or bring a unique perspective. This isn't about mimicking others but finding the distinct angle only you can bring to a crowded field.

Pillar 3: Differentiation: The Heart of What Makes You Irreplaceable

Differentiation is the soul of your UVP and is the quality that makes you unforgettable in a crowd. It requires a willingness to be vulnerable and to share the parts of your story that reveal why you do what you do. After all, this isn't just about competence, but connection with others.

Personal branding expert at Stanford University, Dr. Jennifer Aaker[7] emphasizes that successful brands balance competence with warmth. Think about your own brand. What part of your experience (your personal journey, your values, or even your struggles) makes your UVP unique?

Practical Steps to Articulate Your Differentiation

Find Your Niche: This niche could be a unique expertise, a rare skill set, or a problem-solving approach. For instance, maybe you're a coach. *But what is your niche? Fitness, building a YouTube channel, setting up a nonprofit?*

Leverage Your Story: Share the journey that brought you here. *Did you overcome a challenge that now shapes your perspective? Did a pivotal experience drive your commitment to your work?* Storytelling adds layers to your UVP, combining personal and professional elements.

Highlight Tangible Results: Numbers tell a story too. Think of specific, quantifiable achievements that illustrate your impact. Instead of saying, "I'm good at leading sustainability initiatives," say, "I led a waste reduction program that cut landfill contributions by 35% in one year, helping my organization align with its zero-waste commitment."

Bridging the Practical and the Personal

Your UVP is the story of who you are and the unique impact you make, not just a list of accomplishments. Tangible results anchor your UVP in credibility, but it's the personal dimension that breathes life into it. In a world where personal branding is becoming as vital as technical expertise, your story is what transforms a set of numbers into a meaningful narrative.

People don't just want to know what you've done. They want to understand *how you work* and *why it matters.*

Imagine the difference between reading a fact and hearing a story. A fact might tell you that someone increased customer retention by 20%. A story, however, will show how they listened to frustrated clients, identified overlooked needs, and created a tailored solution that made customers feel valued. The fact catches attention, but the story lingers.

Your UVP should work in the same way. *For example, did your ability to streamline operations come from a knack for pattern recognition that started with solving puzzles as a child? Did your innovative campaign come from challenging the status quo?*

Incorporating your personal story into your UVP shows how your results reflect the qualities that make you, *you.* When people understand the reason behind your success, they don't just see what you've done, they can imagine what you're capable of achieving next.

As we move forward, think about how your personal values amplify your achievements. *How does your story elevate your results from impressive to irreplaceable? And most importantly, how can you craft a UVP that feels like an undeniable extension of your purpose?*

A Refined UVP Framework

Here's a way to think about your UVP that goes beyond the standard formula. Ask yourself these questions:

Who do I serve? Define your audience specifically. Not just "organizations" but "healthcare providers committed to compassionate patient care" or "nonprofits striving for sustainable impact."

What is the impact I create? Consider the change, improvement, or growth that your work brings. Avoid vague terms and focus on specifics, such as measurable outcomes or changes in perspective.

What's my "why"? This is the heart of your UVP and the reason behind your work. If it's sustainability, is it because you want to see a healthier world for the next generation? If it's community engagement, is it because you believe in the power of collective voices? Your why gives your UVP its depth.

UVP = I help [who] achieve [what] by leveraging my [core strength/approach], driven by my commitment to [why].

Figure 3.2 A UVP Framework.

When you put it all together, your UVP becomes a statement of what you do and a vision for the impact you create. Figure 3.2 shows the elements of your UVP.

Examples of UVPs That Feel Like Purposeful Statements

A strong UVP goes beyond mere qualifications to reflect purpose and personality. Here are examples that show how specific language can make a UVP resonate:

1 "I support healthcare providers in delivering compassionate, data-informed patient care by combining my analytical skills with my deep respect for the patient experience, positioning me as a bridge between data and humanity in healthcare."
2 "I help mission-driven startups grow sustainably by blending financial acumen with narrative strategy, making me a unique partner for companies that value both profit and purpose."

Each of these UVPs communicates who the person serves, the impact they bring, and why they are uniquely suited for that role. It feels personal and specific, crafted to reach a distinct audience while reflecting the individual's values and strengths.

I met Elena when I was a founding member of a global NGO. She had spent years working in nonprofit advocacy, helping organizations secure funding and craft impactful campaigns. But when asked to articulate her UVP, she defaulted to vague descriptions: "I help nonprofits succeed."

It wasn't until she reflected on her audience, impact, and why she was passionate about her work that her UVP came into focus.

Elena realized her strength was bridging the gap between grassroots storytelling and donor engagement. Her "why" was rooted in her upbringing. Elena's parents were organizers who struggled to gain traction because they lacked the resources to tell their story effectively.

Elena's refined UVP became: "I help grassroots nonprofits amplify their stories to secure sustainable funding, using my expertise in campaign strategy and my passion for driving social impact."

This shift helped Elena communicate her value with clarity and authenticity, opening doors to larger opportunities.

Finding the Heart of Your UVP

Your UVP is a declaration of who you are and the unique change only you can bring to the world. It's more than a professional tagline. It's a promise. A promise not just to your audience, but to yourself. At its core, a UVP driven by purpose is a statement that grounds you, especially when the path feels difficult or unclear. It's a reminder of why you started and why you keep showing up, day after day.

I'll never forget the moment this became clear to me. I was sitting in yet another meeting, surrounded by talented people discussing compliance updates. The work mattered but I felt hollow, disengaged. I wasn't bored because the work lacked value. I was bored because I realized I wasn't there to tick boxes or file reports. My purpose was deeper.

That realization hit me like a flood. I wasn't just a compliance professional. I was there to empower purpose-driven leaders who wanted to create meaningful work and lead with integrity. I believed in building workplaces and communities where people could thrive, where leadership wasn't just a title but a commitment to positive change. It was this clarity that gave rise to my idea, which I called *Purpose Pathfinders*, even though it would be years before I pressed the button to execute it.

And that's the thing: it didn't matter that I didn't act immediately. What mattered was that I understood what truly motivated me.

That purpose reshaped everything. It influenced how I approached my career, how I led my teams, and how I showed up. It wasn't always easy, but having that clarity gave me the resilience to push forward, even when the path wasn't straightforward.

Your UVP is not about perfection or pleasing everyone. When you find the heart of your UVP, you'll discover it's not just a professional tool. It's the foundation of your purpose and the force that propels you to create the change only you can deliver.

This is especially true if you work in a profession or industry that, let's say, isn't sexy or cool. It gets tiring to keep your energy and enthusiasm when it feels like a grind and you're wondering whether people will listen or if they even care. But when *you know* what your purpose is, and your UVP, it makes things just that bit easier.

One thing I find helpful is to keep your UVP close to you. Maybe you want to put it as a screensaver on your phone or computer. Or print it out and put it in your wallet so you can pull it out when you doubt yourself the most. Remind yourself of what *only you can bring* to work, the community, and the world.

I remember coaching Drew, a mechanical engineer who had spent years designing systems for manufacturing plants. At first, his description of his work sounded clinical and transactional: "I optimize machinery to increase efficiency." It was technically accurate but lacked the spark of someone genuinely connected to their deeper purpose. Something about it felt unfinished, even to him.

As we talked, Drew began reflecting on his early career. One memory emerged that he hadn't revisited in years. He spoke of a skilled machine operator colleague who had been injured in a preventable accident. The injury was severe enough to keep his colleague out of work for months and to cast a long shadow over their team.

At the time, Drew felt an overwhelming mix of emotions: guilt, frustration, and a gnawing sense of responsibility. "I designed that system," he told me. "I didn't think about the human side of it. I was so focused on efficiency that I missed what mattered most: keeping people safe."

That moment became a turning point for him. In the following months after the incident, he poured himself into redesigning the equipment, ensuring efficiency and safety. But it wasn't just the machinery that changed, it was Drew's entire approach to his work. He began asking different questions: *Who's going to use this system? What risks are they taking? How can I protect them while still delivering results?*

As Drew recounted this story, I could see the shift in him. That memory became the foundation of the deeper *why* behind his career. He realized his role wasn't simply to make machines run better but to ensure that every worker who interacted with them went home safe.

His UVP evolved to reflect this newfound clarity: "I design systems that increase efficiency while prioritizing worker safety, ensuring manufacturing teams can work smarter and safer every day."

For Drew, it wasn't about being just another engineer. It was about being the kind of leader who put people first, transforming workplaces not just through better machinery but through a deeper commitment to those who relied on it.

Your Compass for Meaningful Impact

Uncovering your "why" is the foundation of a purposeful and impactful career. At its core, a UVP is both a compass and a bridge. It helps you navigate the often murky waters of career decisions, aligning your actions with your deeper purpose. At the same time, it connects you to the people, organizations, and opportunities that resonate with your vision. When your UVP is grounded in purpose, it creates a magnetic pull that draws the right opportunities toward you.

A purpose-driven UVP is transformative because it speaks to something universal: the human desire for meaning. People are drawn to authenticity and clarity, especially when it is tied to a deeper cause. When you write your UVP in a way that reflects not just your skills but the change you're here to create, you naturally attract others who also share that vision.

Purpose-driven work isn't easy. It often comes with uncertainty, setbacks, and moments of doubt. This is where your UVP becomes invaluable. In those challenging moments, it reminds you of the bigger picture: *This is why I started. This is why it matters.*

To refine your UVP into a tool for clarity and resilience, consider these questions:

Does this reflect the legacy I want to leave?

Does it align with the impact I want to create in the world?

When your UVP is built on a foundation of purpose, it transforms into a mission that shapes your decisions, energizes your efforts, and inspires you to keep moving forward.

As you move into the next chapter, remember that your UVP is a powerful tool, but its true potential lies in how you use it. Chapter 4 is about turning intention into action, and recognizing when it's time to step boldly into the uncertainty that often accompanies growth.

Notes

1 Grant, A. 2017. *Originals: How Non-Conformists Move the World.* Penguin Books.
2 Seligman, M. E. P. 2011. *Learned Optimism: How to Change Your Mind and Your Life.* Vintage.
3 Clifton, D. O., C. Anderson, and L. A. Schreiner. 2016. *StrengthsQuest: Discover and Develop Your Strengths in Academics, Career, and Beyond.* Gallup Press.
4 Gallup. n.d. "CliftonStrengths." *Gallup.* Accessed 13 February 2025. https://www.gallup.com/cliftonstrengths/en/strengthsfinder.aspx.
5 VIA Institute on Character. n.d. "VIA Character Strengths." *VIA Institute on Character.* Accessed 13 February 2025. https://www.viacharacter.org/.
6 Sinek, S. 2019. *The Infinite Game.* Penguin Random House.
7 Aaker, J. L., E. N. Garbinsky, and K. D. Vohs. 2012. "Cultivating Admiration in Brands: Warmth, Competence, and Landing in the 'Golden Quadrant.'" *Journal of Consumer Psychology* 22(2): 191–194. https://doi.org/10.1016/j.jcps.2011.11.012.

Chapter 4

Bold Moves, Bold Lives

It was one of those golden Sydney afternoons where the light sparkled off the water like something out of a dream. I'd just returned home from work – my office overlooked the breathtaking Sydney Harbour, a view that always felt like a privilege.

My daily routine was its own kind of magic. I walked across the Sydney Harbour Bridge to work most days, soaking in the fresh sea air. Sometimes, I'd hop on a bus to meet with my professors at the University of New South Wales, where we would try and figure out how to make sense of the data I'd collected for my PhD. Weekends were spent at the beaches or exploring the wineries, creating a rhythm of life that felt effortless and full.

It was 2003. I was thriving in my career. My transition from academia into corporate roles at McDonald's and then Coca-Cola Amatil had propelled me to new heights, giving me a sense of momentum and accomplishment. I'd worked hard to build something meaningful, and I was proud of what I'd achieved.

Nigel, my husband, was thriving too. We often talked about our dreams for the future. The adventures we wanted to take and the possibilities that lay ahead. But life, as it does, threw us an unexpected twist.

That day, when Nigel walked through the door of our early 20th-century terrace, his face lit with a mixture of excitement and nerves.

"They want me in Chicago," he said, holding out a letter from McDonald's. A transfer to their global headquarters.

His words hung in the air. Chicago. The United States. It was the opportunity of a lifetime, and I could see in his expression how much it meant to him.

But for me, it wasn't a simple yes. I was in the early stages of pregnancy with our first child, and the future felt both full of promise and overwhelming uncertainty. A new life was growing inside me, and the prospect of starting over in a new country felt like leaping into the unknown on every possible level.

DOI: 10.4324/9781003627265-5

Why would anyone want to swap this idyllic life for something so uncertain?

We had a home we were renovating, friends who were our second family, and a routine that felt perfect. My career was on an upward trajectory, and I had finally found my rhythm. Yet, deep down, I knew that boldness and comfort rarely coexist. Something inside me whispered that this was a moment to lean into courage, even if fear and doubt were loud in my mind.

The decision to leave Sydney wasn't easy. It meant walking away from the tangible and the known for something intangible and unknown: the hope of what could be. It meant stepping into a new chapter, not just as a professional but as a soon-to-be mother, ready to redefine what success and fulfillment looked like.

Looking back, that moment marked the beginning of a profound lesson in boldness. It's not about abandoning fear but learning to walk with it. It's about trusting that the life waiting for you on the other side of uncertainty is worth the leap.

This chapter is a guide to boldness, offering tools, stories, and reflections to help you step forward into your next chapter. Whether your leap involves switching industries, pursuing a new role, or starting a business, this is your roadmap to living a bold and purposeful life.

What Does It Mean to Be Bold?

Boldness gets a lot of hype. It's often mistaken for fearlessness. As if bold people charge ahead without hesitation, untouched by doubt.

But that's not how it works.

Boldness is stepping forward even when uncertainty lingers, when the stakes feel high, and when the little voice in your head whispers, *Are you sure?*

It's not about eliminating fear, but rather ensuring it doesn't dictate our actions.

After all, boldness shows up in different ways.

In **leadership**, it's making tough decisions, challenging the status quo, and speaking up when it's easier to stay quiet.

In **personal growth**, it's trying new things, leaning into discomfort, and betting on yourself. Even when there are no guarantees.

In **communication**, it's owning your voice, saying what needs to be said, and standing firm in your truth.

In **career moves**, it's taking strategic risks, stepping into rooms that intimidate you, and chasing opportunities that feel just out of reach.

At its core, boldness is about choosing action over hesitation and trusting that you'll figure it out along the way.

When I think back to our move to Chicago, boldness didn't mean I had everything mapped out. It wasn't about marching forward with unshakable confidence. It was about taking one step at a time. Led by purpose, resilience, and the belief that I could build something meaningful from scratch.

The 3C Model of Boldness

At the heart of every bold move, whether it's speaking up in a boardroom, making a life-changing career pivot, or standing firm in your truth, lies the **3C Model of Boldness: Clarity** (the foundation), **Courage** (the engine), **and Commitment** (the glue). Let's break them down.

1 **Clarity: The Foundation of Boldness**

Boldness starts with knowing who you are, what you stand for, and what you refuse to compromise on. Without that foundation, boldness is just impulsivity, jumping from one thing to the next without direction. I learned this the hard way.

Years ago, I sat across from a hiring manager at one of the world's biggest companies. The job was a step up. The kind of position that could open all the right doors. On paper, it made sense. It was the logical next move in my career.

But something felt off.

I couldn't shake the feeling that I was being pulled toward a different path. One that wasn't written in a job description. One that didn't come with a neatly paved roadmap.

I had a choice. I could take the job, follow the script, and stay in the safe zone. Or I could listen to the part of me that knew I was meant for something different.

That was the moment I realized: boldness isn't about taking risks just for the sake of it. It's about taking the right risks. And you can only do that when you're clear on what matters.

The clearest people in the world don't waste time on decisions that aren't meant for them. They know what fits and what doesn't. They don't chase opportunities. They choose them.

That's the kind of clarity that builds bold careers. Not just knowing what you want, but knowing what you won't tolerate.

Clarity makes boldness easier. Because when you're clear, the right path isn't a mystery, it's a decision.

2 **Courage: The Engine of Boldness**

Clarity is knowing where you're headed. Courage is the moment you step forward despite the fear.

Most people think courage is about being fearless. It's not.

It's about taking action while the fear still lingers.

I'll never forget the first time I sat at a leadership table with executives who had built billion-dollar companies. They were the type of people who made decisions that moved markets, who spoke in numbers and strategy like they were second nature, and who carried a quiet confidence that said, *I belong here.*

I took my seat, but my mind was already racing. I had spent my career mastering my craft, leading teams, and driving change. I knew the data, understood the risks, and had a clear perspective on the challenges ahead. But as I looked around the room, I felt something else creeping in. Doubt.

Not because I wasn't capable. Not because I didn't have something valuable to say. But because the room itself had a way of making you question your own presence in it. The conversations moved fast, filled with assumptions and shorthand that only people who had been in those rooms for years could easily decode. I watched as they exchanged glances, nodding in sync, effortlessly bouncing off one another's ideas. And at that moment, I had a choice.

I could shrink back, waiting for permission to speak. Or I could decide that my voice belonged, whether they expected it or not.

I took a breath. Leaned in. And when the opportunity opened, I spoke. Not just to fill space, not just to prove I had a seat at the table, but to say something that mattered. Something that shifted the conversation.

The room went quiet for half a second. That heartbeat of hesitation before someone acknowledged, *That's a good point.*

And just like that, I realized something that changed everything.

The people in these rooms weren't necessarily the smartest, the most qualified, or even the most innovative. They were simply the ones who decided to be there. The ones who understood that boldness wasn't about waiting for someone to validate your worth. It was about owning it yourself.

That day, something clicked for me. I stopped assuming that presence was something you earned after enough years of experience, enough credentials, enough proving yourself. I started seeing it for what it really was: a choice. A moment-to-moment decision to either lean in or fade back.

And once I saw it, I couldn't unsee it.

It wasn't just in executive meetings. It was in every career move I made, every high-stakes conversation, every bold step forward. The leaders who shaped industries, the ones who commanded rooms and drove change, weren't always the loudest or the most charismatic. But they carried a kind of certainty, an unshakable belief that they belonged. And because they believed it, others did too.

Because here's the truth no one tells you. Boldness is what separates those who influence the room from those who are just sitting in it.

That's not to say boldness is easy. It's not. It takes practice. It takes choosing, over and over again, to push through discomfort, to raise your hand, to trust that what you have to say is worth hearing.

And sometimes, boldness means speaking. Other times, it means staying in the room long enough to shape the conversation.

It means not letting the speed of the discussion convince you that you have nothing to add. It means recognizing that silence, when used with intention, can be just as powerful as words. It means understanding that leadership isn't about knowing all the answers. It's about having the conviction to ask the right questions.

I think about that first meeting often. About the way I almost let self-doubt take me out of the conversation before I even opened my mouth. About the way, a single moment of boldness shifted how I saw myself in every room that came after.

Because the real lesson that day wasn't about that meeting. It was about how I chose to show up.

And that's the lesson I carry with me and the lesson I hope to pass on.

You don't wait for permission to be bold. You decide. And once you do, everything changes.

The first bold step is always the hardest. But once you take it, something changes. You start to realize that fear is just a feeling, not a barrier.

Courage in careers looks different for everyone.

It's the person who finally asks for the raise they know they deserve.

It's the leader who challenges an outdated approach in a meeting full of skeptics.

It's the entrepreneur who launches something before they feel fully ready.

Courage is the thing that separates those who watch from the sidelines from those who step into the game.

If you're waiting for fear to disappear before you act, you'll be waiting forever. The boldest people in the world aren't fearless. They just move forward anyway.

3 Commitment: The Glue of Boldness

Starting something bold is one thing. Sticking with it when things get hard is another. This is the part no one talks about.

People love the idea of boldness when it's exciting. When the possibilities feel endless. When everything is fresh and new. But bold moves aren't made in a single moment.

They're built in the in-between.

The late nights when progress feels slow.

The weeks when doubt creeps back in.

The moments when no one else can see the vision but you.

I felt it when I left behind a stable career path to chase something that had no guarantees. I felt it when I started writing my book and realized it was far harder than I expected. I felt it when I built my business from scratch, without a safety net, without a clear roadmap.

Boldness isn't just about having the guts to start. It's about having the grit to keep going.

Angela Duckworth,[1] in her groundbreaking research on grit, defines it as the combination of passion and perseverance over the long haul. The difference between those who succeed and those who quit isn't talent, intelligence, or luck. It's staying in the game long enough to see it through.

I think about the nights I stared at my laptop, my book manuscript blinking back at me, a mess of unfinished thoughts that felt nowhere near the book I had envisioned. The excitement of the first few chapters had faded, replaced by the grind of rewriting, restructuring, and second-guessing everything. The easy thing would have been to set it aside, to convince myself that now wasn't the right time, that I'd come back to it when inspiration struck again.

But grit isn't about inspiration. It's about showing up anyway.

So I did.

Word by word. Edit by edit. Line by line.

Even when the words didn't flow. Even when the vision felt blurry.

This is what boldness actually looks like – not the big, cinematic leap, but the quiet, relentless refusal to quit.

The leaders who truly make an impact – the ones who shape industries, build movements, and create lasting change – aren't the ones who had a single bold moment. They're the ones who had a thousand small moments of sticking with it.

Elon Musk has spoken about how SpaceX was weeks away from bankruptcy[2] before they landed their first successful launch. J. K. Rowling was rejected 12 times before someone took a chance on Harry Potter.[3]

What separates them from everyone else?

They kept going.

Because commitment isn't about motivation. Motivation fades. Commitment stays.

I remember the day I signed my first big client after starting my own business. It didn't happen overnight. There were months of work before that moment – days of refining my message, testing ideas, and learning from failure. I could have stopped at any point. The doubt, the fear, and the uncertainty were all very real.

But I didn't – because I knew something that every bold leader comes to understand:

Success is just persistence in disguise.

Commitment is waking up every morning and choosing to stay the course. It's working toward a vision that only exists in your mind until, one day, it doesn't.

So if you're in that place right now – the messy middle, the slow grind, and the frustrating in-between – don't stop.

Your bold move isn't just about the moment you start. It's about the moment you choose (again and again) to keep going.

Boldness doesn't belong to the most talented. It belongs to those who are willing to stay the course.

And if you're willing to keep showing up, even when no one's watching, that's when the game truly changes.

The world belongs to the bold. Not because they're fearless. Not because they're lucky.

But because they know what they want, take action despite the fear, and commit to seeing it through.

If you want to lead, grow, and make an impact, you need all three.

Without clarity, you'll chase the wrong goals.

Without courage, you'll stay stuck in hesitation.

Without commitment, you'll give up before you see the results.

Clarity. Courage. Commitment.

This is how bold careers are built. This is how bold leaders are made. And this is how you create a life you're truly proud of.

From Boldness to Alignment

Boldness isn't just about making a move. It's about making the right move because not every risk is worth taking, and not every opportunity is a good fit.

The boldest people aren't the ones who say yes to everything. They're the ones who have the clarity to know what aligns with their strengths, the courage to pursue it, and the commitment to see it through.

And this is where your unique value proposition (UVP) from Chapter 3 becomes a game-changer. Your UVP isn't just a tagline or a polished elevator pitch. It's a strategic filter. It helps you cut through the noise, eliminate distractions, and focus on opportunities that truly align with your values and strengths. It turns boldness into something sustainable.

Illuminating the Path Forward

When standing at the edge of a bold career move, it's easy to get lost in the possibilities, to feel pulled in a hundred directions at once. The rush of excitement can cloud your judgment, making every option look appealing, especially those that offer immediate rewards. The promise of a title, a bigger paycheck, or a new challenge can be tempting. But boldness without alignment is just impulsivity.

That's where a clear UVP becomes a guiding force. It acts like a flashlight in the fog, cutting through short-term distractions and illuminating the opportunities that actually make sense for who you are and where you want to go.

Career decisions anchored in intrinsic motivation lead to greater long-term satisfaction and success.[4] [5] When a career move is aligned with what truly matters to you (your strengths, your impact, and your values) it's not just another job but a step toward something more meaningful, something that sustains and energizes you rather than drains you over time.

I once coached Jessica, a marketing executive at a corporate firm, who was torn between staying in her comfortable role or taking a leap into the unpredictable world of startups. She was drawn to the energy and innovation of a fast-moving environment, but she hesitated. The risk felt enormous.

It wasn't until she articulated her UVP – *I bring creativity and strategic insight to help early-stage companies establish compelling brand identities* – that the path forward became clear. She could see, in black and white, where she thrived and where she could make the biggest impact. When she made the leap, she didn't just take any startup role. She chose one that aligned perfectly with her unique strengths.

It's easy to convince yourself that boldness means moving quickly, saying yes, and figuring it out later. But true boldness is discerning. It's the ability to look at an opportunity and say, *Is this right for me? Does this allow me to do what I do best? Is this move aligned with the future I'm building, or is it just a distraction?*

Fueling Confidence in the Face of Self-Doubt

Even when the path is clear, stepping forward can feel impossible. The mind fills with questions. *What if I fail? What if I don't belong? What if I'm not ready?* This is the part of boldness that no one talks about – the way uncertainty creeps in, even when everything logically points to the right decision.

Confidence isn't about eliminating those thoughts. It's about having something stronger to hold onto when they appear. That's what a UVP does. It becomes an anchor, a constant reminder of your value, your strengths, and the impact you bring.

People with a strong internal sense of self-efficacy, the belief in their own ability to succeed, are the ones who thrive in times of uncertainty.[6] And that belief isn't something that just appears. It's reinforced by the way you define your strengths and the way you remind yourself of what you bring to the table.

I know this firsthand. I've already told you that I was 36 weeks pregnant when I boarded the plane headed from Sydney to Chicago. I'd taken a 12-month leave of absence from my job in Australia, to settle into motherhood and a new country. As the harsh Chicago winter moved into Spring and then Summer, I began asking myself *what's next?*

But with no job, no professional network, and no roadmap, I felt the weight of uncertainty pressing in on me every day. It would have been easy to shrink myself, to take whatever opportunity came my way just to gain a sense of security. But I reminded myself, over and over again, that I wasn't just someone looking for work. I had something valuable to offer. And that's what gave me the confidence to show up in networking conversations differently. It reminded me that I wasn't there to beg for an opportunity, I was there to find the right fit.

Without that sense of clarity, it would have been easy to let imposter syndrome take over, to convince myself that I wasn't qualified enough, connected enough, or ready enough. But confidence doesn't come from the absence of doubt. It comes from choosing to believe in yourself, even when the fear is present.

That's why clarity matters. Because when you know exactly what you bring to the table, doubt may still whisper, but it won't have the final word.

Not Every Bold Move Is the Right Move

There's a myth that boldness means saying yes to everything. That every opportunity that knocks should be welcomed. But the truth is, not every bold move is the right move. Some doors lead to paths that look exciting at first but pull you further away from who you are.

That's because external motivators, whether money, prestige, or social expectations, often lead to burnout and disengagement when they don't align with personal values.[7] [8] [9] [10] The most successful careers aren't just about chasing opportunities. They're about choosing the right ones.

I've seen so many people take leaps that looked bold on the outside – quitting their jobs, switching industries, and moving to new cities – only to realize that they had built a new version of the same dissatisfaction they were trying to escape.

Because they hadn't paused to ask the deeper question: *Does this align with the way I work best?*

A fulfilling career isn't just about what you do, it's also about how you do it. There are five core principles that shape long-term career satisfaction.[11] People thrive when:

1 They feel connected to others.
2 They have autonomy in their work.
3 They feel competent in their role.

4 They are in a positive work environment.
5 Their work has meaning.

A bold career move that doesn't take these factors into account may seem thrilling at first, but over time, the cracks will show.

That's why alignment isn't just about external fit, it's also about internal fulfillment. Research by Kennon and Kasser[12] reinforces this idea, showing that people experience the highest levels of fulfillment when they focus on goals rooted in growth, connection, and contribution. Not external markers like status or financial success.

When we first framed a UVP in Chapter 3, we structured it as: *I help [who] achieve [what] by leveraging my [core strength/approach], driven by my commitment to [why].*

But bold career moves require more than just looking outward. They demand looking inward, understanding not just who you serve, but what makes you thrive.

Before making any major move, it's worth taking a step back. Instead of asking, *Is this bold?* ask, *Is this right?* Because sometimes, the boldest thing you can do isn't leaping into something new. Sometimes, the boldest thing you can do is walking away from something that isn't meant for you.

Because boldness, the kind that creates real, meaningful change, isn't about movement for the sake of movement. It's about *alignment.*

Alignment with your values.

Alignment with your strengths.

Alignment with the kind of life you want to build.

Without that foundation, bold moves turn into reckless experiments. Exciting at first, but ultimately exhausting and unsustainable.

With it, bold moves become something else entirely: intentional, powerful, and deeply fulfilling. The question isn't whether you should take bold steps. It's whether those steps are leading you toward something worth building.

There are five elements that determine whether a bold career move will serve you in the long run. These aren't just theoretical ideas but are the non-negotiables that influence whether your career decisions lead to growth, success, and personal fulfillment or whether they pull you into roles and environments that drain you.

If you're considering a bold move, pay attention to these. They will determine whether your next step is a breakthrough or a detour.

1 **The Power of Connection: Who You Surround Yourself with Matters**

No one builds a bold career alone. At every pivotal moment in my journey, every risk I took, every opportunity I pursued, every challenge I faced, there were people standing beside me. Mentors who helped me see beyond my doubts. Colleagues who pushed me to step up. Friends who reminded me why I started in the first place.

Connection isn't just a nice-to-have in your career. It's essential. Feeling connected to others is one of the three fundamental psychological needs that drive motivation and well-being.

When considering a bold move, your connections can be the difference between leaping with confidence and holding yourself back. If you feel stuck, ask yourself: *Who am I surrounding myself with? Who lifts me up? Who challenges me to think bigger? Who helps me push through uncertainty?*

And just as importantly, where are the gaps? If you don't yet have mentors, colleagues, or peers who can guide and support you, this is your invitation to start building those relationships. The boldest people in the world don't move alone. They move with a powerful network behind and beside them.

2 **Autonomy: The Freedom to Own Your Career**

There is nothing more stifling than waking up every morning knowing that no matter how hard you work, how sharp your ideas are, or how much potential you bring, your decisions will still be run through layers of approval. The spark of creativity, dimmed by bureaucracy. The fire of ambition, dulled by a culture of hesitation.

It's a slow erosion, one that doesn't happen overnight. At first, you tell yourself it's just part of the process. That red tape is normal. That playing by the rules will eventually lead to recognition. But over time, something shifts. You stop offering ideas because you already know they'll be dismissed. You stop pushing for innovation because it's easier to conform. You start to shrink within your own career, not because you lack ability, but because the system around you refuses to let you expand.

Autonomy isn't about working alone. It's about having the freedom to bring your best ideas to life. To take ownership of your work. To make decisions without waiting for approval from people who don't understand your expertise. Autonomy is what transforms a job into something bigger, a platform for impact.

You've probably felt this way yourself. When you're trusted to make decisions, shape your work, and drive results on your own terms, you feel more engaged, more creative, and more successful. The opposite is also true. When autonomy is stripped away, performance declines. You don't want to take risks. Some people even stop caring and do just enough to survive, but never enough to thrive.

I once worked with a business strategist named Alan. A talented guy with a mind built for innovation. But he was stuck under a boss who saw every decision as a threat to their own control. No matter what Alan proposed, it had to be approved, adjusted, and diluted before it ever saw the light of day. He wasn't just being managed, he was being suffocated.

Then, an opportunity came. A lateral move to a different department. No big title change. No immediate raise. Just a shift into a team where he would have more autonomy.

At first, he hesitated. *Wouldn't it be a step backward? Wouldn't it make more sense to wait for a real promotion?*

But when he looked at the reality of his current role, the frustration, the lack of trust, and the way it drained his energy, he realized something critical: staying in the wrong environment was far riskier than stepping into the unknown.

So, he took the move.

Within six months, he was leading major projects. A year later, he was promoted. Not because he chased a title, but because he put himself in a space where he could finally breathe, create, and contribute at his highest level.

This is what autonomy does. It creates momentum. It shifts a career from passive to active, from reactive to intentional. It fuels the kind of leadership that is built not on compliance, but on ownership.

If you're considering a bold move, don't just ask yourself, *Is this a better title?* or *Is this a bigger paycheck?* Ask yourself, *Will this give me the freedom to do my best work?*

Because a bold move that locks you into the wrong structure isn't bold at all.

It's a cage with a different name.

3 Competence: The Confidence That Comes from Mastery

The world doesn't just open doors for those who wait patiently outside. It opens for those who step forward and believe they belong inside.

And that belief? It doesn't come from wishful thinking. It comes from competence.

Competence isn't just about ticking off a list of skills or collecting credentials. It's about something deeper, a quiet, unshakable understanding that you bring value. That you are not just filling a role, but actively shaping outcomes. That your ideas don't just exist for validation, they move things forward.

But here's the paradox: most people don't see their own competence.

Instead, they focus on the gaps. The things they haven't mastered yet. The ways they fall short compared to someone more experienced, more established, more seemingly perfect.

I see it all the time: wonderful, capable professionals who hesitate. Who second-guess themselves. Who convince themselves they need one more certification, one more year of experience, and one more piece of proof before they take the leap.

But the truth is, growth doesn't come from waiting until you feel fully ready.

It comes from stepping into roles that stretch you.

When I transitioned into a leadership role at a Fortune 500 company, I had moments where I felt out of my depth. I walked into meetings where people spoke about financial models I hadn't heard of, in strategy frameworks I hadn't been trained on. But instead of focusing on what I lacked, I reminded myself of what I already knew: how to solve complex problems, how to lead teams through uncertainty, and how to drive real results.

And here's what I learned: most people are making it up as they go.

The executives you admire, the industry leaders who seem so confident? They weren't handed a manual with all the answers. They stepped into challenges before they felt completely ready, and they figured it out.

That's what real competence is. Not just knowledge. Not just skill. But the belief that you can handle whatever comes next.

So before you take a bold leap, take stock of yourself. *What are the strengths that make you uniquely valuable? What are the skills that set you apart? And most importantly: does this move challenge you in a way that fuels your growth rather than overwhelms it?*

Because the best bold moves? They're the ones that force you to level up.

4 **The Emotional Climate: The Unseen Force That Shapes Your Career**

You can have everything on paper – the perfect title, the impressive salary, and the kind of job that looks like success from the outside.

But what if the emotional climate is toxic?

If you wake up every morning with a sense of dread?

If the energy in the room makes you question your worth instead of amplifying it?

Then, no title, no boatload of options, and no prestige will be enough.

Culture matters. The way leaders engage matters. The people you surround yourself with? They will shape your future more than any job description ever could.

I think of a leader I once worked with. A powerhouse in her industry, known for her strategic mind and ability to turn struggling teams into high-performing ones. When she landed a role at one of the most well-respected companies in her field, it felt like a career-defining moment. Everything about the job made sense. On paper. The company's reputation was stellar, the compensation was more than she had ever earned, and the role itself promised influence, impact, and a chance to lead at the highest level.

But six months in, something was wrong.

She wasn't struggling with the work. She knew how to navigate complex challenges. She wasn't doubting her abilities, after all, she had a proven track record. But something about the energy in the room drained her. The unspoken expectations. The culture of constant comparison. The pressure to perform instead of connect. It was a place where vulnerability was seen as weakness, where no one admitted when they were struggling, and where leadership meant always having the answer. Never the question. She did everything right. But she never felt right.

That's the part of bold career moves that doesn't get talked about. The fact that you can land the "dream job" and still feel like an outsider in the space that was supposed to elevate you.

Eventually, she made another bold move. She left. Not because she wasn't capable, but because she refused to shrink herself to fit into a culture that didn't align with who she was or how she led.

This is what people miss when they make bold moves. They get caught up in the title, the company name, and the perceived prestige. But they forget to ask the deeper questions.

What does this culture feel like?

Are these people driven by collaboration or competition?

Do they support each other or silently undercut one another?

Is failure seen as part of growth or as something to be punished?

Because no matter how bold you are, your environment will shape you. And a bold move that places you in the wrong emotional climate? That's not a move forward. That's a slow unraveling of everything that makes you great.

5 The Deepest Driver of Bold Moves: Meaning

At the end of the day, bold moves that lack meaning are just … moves.

They might look good on paper. But if they don't align with something deeper, something that fuels you, they eventually lose their shine.

Amy Wrzesniewski's research on career orientation shows that people experience work in three ways: as a job, a career, or a calling.[13] A job is a means to an end, a way to pay the bills. A career is about progression, achievement, and climbing the ladder. But a calling? A calling is something else entirely. It's when work becomes an extension of who you are. When what you do isn't just about external rewards, but about the impact it allows you to have.

And those who experience work as a calling? They don't just perform better. They are more fulfilled, more resilient, and more successful in the long run.

That's because meaning is what keeps you going when things get hard. It's what makes the risk worth it. It's what stops you from quitting when the path gets steep, when progress feels slow, when every logical part of you wonders if you should take the easier route.

Abraham Maslow once wrote, "The most beautiful fate, the most wonderful good fortune that can happen to any human being, is to be paid for doing that which he passionately loves to do."

And yet, so many people spend their careers chasing security instead of purpose. Choosing roles that feel safe over ones that feel right. Convincing themselves that passion is a luxury, that meaning is something they'll prioritize later.

But here's the truth: later never comes. You don't stumble into meaningful work by accident. You choose it. You make the bold move that brings you closer to it.

And meaning doesn't always mean a dramatic reinvention. Sometimes, it's about shifting how you show up in the work you already do. Sometimes, it's about saying yes to a project that excites you or stepping into a leadership role that allows you to create change in a way that matters.

So if you're considering a bold move, ask yourself: *Does this bring me closer to the work that matters most to me? Does this align with the kind of impact I want to have?*

Because the boldest move you can make isn't about titles, status, or recognition. It's the move that leads you toward the work you were meant to do.

And that?

That changes everything.

The Full Picture of Boldness

For so long, we've been taught to measure success by the things we can list on a résumé: titles, promotions, salaries, and industry recognition. The corner office. The leadership role. The big win that makes everything look impressive from the outside. But if boldness was only about external success, why do so many people reach the peak of their careers and still feel unfulfilled?

Because bold moves, at their core, aren't just about what you do. They're about who you become in the process.

When we started this chapter, we talked about your UVP – the way you articulate your impact in the world. At first glance, it might seem like a formula: a way to position yourself in the job market, a way to stand out. It answers the external question: *What do you do?* But bold career moves demand something more. They don't just require you to understand your value in the marketplace. They require you to align that value with the right version of yourself.

Because a career that looks successful on the outside but drains you from the inside? That's not success at all.

This is the part of boldness that most people miss. It's easy to assume that making a bold move means chasing something bigger, shinier, and more visible. *But real boldness?* It's having the courage to say no to what isn't right. To recognize when an opportunity, no matter how impressive, doesn't align with who you are or what you stand for.

The world will try to pull you toward metrics of success that don't actually matter to you. The bigger title. The executive suite. The golden handcuffs that make it hard to walk away. But before you make any bold move, ask yourself:

Is this opportunity aligned with my core strengths and values?

Will this move contribute to the legacy I want to leave?

Am I making this decision for external validation or internal fulfillment?

Because the boldest moves, the ones that truly transform careers and lives, aren't just about ambition. They are rooted in purpose.

Recognizing When It's Time for a Bold Move

Timing matters.

You can have all the clarity on the world, but if you jump too soon or hold back for too long, your bold move may not land the way you want it to. Recognizing the signs that you're ready for change is just as important as knowing where you want to go.

Sometimes, the signs are obvious. You feel stuck as if you've outgrown your role but don't know where to go next. We talked about this in Chapter 1. You feel disconnected, like the work you're doing no longer excites or challenges you. Or you feel restless, pulled toward something more, even if you can't quite articulate what that *more* is.

Other times, the signals are more subtle. A growing frustration with leadership. A gnawing feeling that your skills aren't being fully used. An awareness that you're playing it safe, coasting on what's comfortable rather than stepping into what's possible.

And then, there's the undeniable pull. That moment when you realize that staying where you are is actually the bigger risk.

My friend Ava had built her career as a structural engineer, working on complex, large-scale projects that required precision, technical expertise, and a deep understanding of risk. She was brilliant at what she did, respected for her ability to see problems before they happened, to innovate solutions others overlooked, and to lead teams through high-stakes decisions.

But something had shifted.

The work that once challenged her now felt routine. The same types of projects. The same constraints. The same feeling that she was solving problems, but not pushing boundaries. She had started to feel invisible in her own career.

For years, Ava had entertained the idea of moving into a more strategic leadership role. She had the expertise. The credibility. The ability to influence the way decisions were made, not just execute them. But every time she considered stepping up, she hesitated.

What if she wasn't ready?

What if she wasn't the kind of leader the company wanted?

What if she failed?

So she stayed where she was. Waiting. Hoping that someone would see her potential and invite her to the table.

Then, one day, she had a conversation that changed everything. A colleague she deeply respected, a senior leader, asked her a simple question:

"Why are you waiting for someone else to tell you you're ready?"

The words hit her like a gut punch. She realized, in that moment, that her hesitation had never been about her capability. It had been about permission. She had been waiting for someone to *choose her* – when all along, she had the power to choose herself.

That clarity changed everything.

Ava stopped waiting for the right moment. She started positioning herself for the role she wanted. She spoke up in executive meetings. She challenged outdated processes. She took on high-visibility projects that allowed her to step beyond the technical details and into strategic decision-making.

And by the time a leadership opportunity officially opened? There was no doubt. She wasn't just a candidate. She was the obvious choice.

This is what people don't always realize about bold moves. They don't always start with a job offer, a promotion, or a new opportunity falling into your lap. Sometimes, they start with a decision. A decision to stop playing small.

If you find yourself constantly questioning whether it's time for a bold move, the answer is probably yes. The real question is: *What's stopping you?*

A Framework for Bold Career Steps

When the moment comes to make a bold move, the instinct is often to go all in. Quit. Pivot. Reinvent everything overnight. The adrenaline of possibility takes over, and it's easy to think that action alone is enough.

But boldness without a plan isn't boldness at all. It's chaos.

The difference between reckless leaps and strategic moves isn't hesitation, it's preparation. Boldness with a strategy? That's where lasting success is built.

Before making any big move, pause. Assess the risk versus the reward.

Boldness doesn't mean ignoring the challenges. It means seeing them clearly and stepping forward anyway. *What do you stand to gain? What's the worst that could happen?*

And perhaps the most important question of all. *What's the cost of staying exactly where you are?*

Growth rarely feels comfortable. It's unsettling, messy, and full of moments where doubt creeps in. But in the long run, staying in a place where you are no longer expanding is far riskier than stepping into the unknown.

Bold Moves Shape Bold Lives

At some point in your career, a moment will come – a moment where you feel the weight of a decision pressing against you, pulling you in two directions. Stay where it's safe – where you know the rules, the expectations, and the comfort of what is familiar. Or, step into the unknown, where nothing is guaranteed but everything is possible.

Every bold move is a crossroads.

It's not just about switching roles, industries, or companies. It's about something bigger. It's about deciding whether you will keep walking a path that no longer excites you or whether you will bet on something greater. Yourself.

The boldest careers, the ones filled with impact, fulfillment, and meaning, aren't built in a single leap. They are built in moments of courage, in choices that stretch you, and in steps that don't always feel easy but are always right.

And bold moves don't stop at career decisions. Because once you make the choice to step forward, something shifts. It's no longer just about *what* you do, it's about how you show up.

The most successful people in the world, the ones who lead, inspire, and drive real change, don't just make bold moves behind the scenes. They own the room. They command the stage. They speak with conviction, carry themselves with authority, and make people stop and listen.

So, if you've been waiting for permission to step up, to be seen, and to take your place at the table. Here it is.

Because the boldest move you will ever make isn't about a job title, a salary, or a promotion.

It's about owning your voice, standing in your power, and stepping fully into the leader you were always meant to be. And that? That's where we go next.

Notes

1 Duckworth, A. 2016. *Grit: The Power of Passion and Perseverance*. Scribner.
2 Kay, G. 2021. "Elon Musk Says SpaceX Faces Bankruptcy Risk Without Starship Raptor Progress." *Business Insider*, November 30. https://www.businessinsider.com/elon-musk-spacex-faces-bankruptcy-risk-without-starship-raptor-progress-2021-11.
3 Millington, A. 2018. "J.K. Rowling's Pitch for 'Harry Potter' Was Rejected 12 Times – Read the Now-Famous Letter Here." *Business Insider*, July 30. https://www.businessinsider.com/revealed-jk-rowlings-original-pitch-for-harry-potter-2017-10.
4 Ryan, R., and E. Deci. 2020. "Intrinsic and Extrinsic Motivation from a Self-Determination Theory Perspective: Definitions, Theory, Practices, and Future Directions." *Contemporary Educational Psychology* 61: 101860. https://doi.org/10.1016/j.cedpsych.2020.101860.
5 Ryan, R., and E. Deci. 2017. *Self-Determination Theory: Basic Psychological Needs in Motivation, Development, and Wellness*. Guilford Press.
6 Zacher, H., and C. W. Rudolph. 2021. "Relationships between Psychological Contract Breach and Employee Well-Being and Career-Related Behavior: The Role of Occupational Future Time Perspective." *Journal of Organizational Behavior* 42(1): 84–99. https://doi.org/10.1002/job.2495.
7 Bryson, A., and G. MacKerron. 2016. "Are You Happy While You Work?" *The Economic Journal* 127(599): 106–125.
8 Schaufeli, W. B., and T. W. Taris. 2014. "A Critical Review of the Job Demands-Resource Model: Implications for Improving Work and Health." In *Bridging Occupational, Organizational and Public Health: A Transdisciplinary Approach*, edited by G. F. Bauer and O. Hammig, 43–68. Springer.
9 Krekel, C., G. Ward, and J.-E. De Neve. 2017. "Employee Wellbeing, Productivity, and Firm Performance: Evidence and Case Studies." In *Global Happiness Policy Report 2019*, edited by the Global Happiness Council, 2019. Sustainable Development Solutions Network.
10 Achor, S., A. Reece, G. Y. Kellerman, and J. Robichaux. 2018. "9 Out of 10 People Are Willing to Earn Less Money to Do More Meaningful Work." *Harvard Business Review*, November 6, 2018. https://hbr.org/2018/11/9-out-of-10-people-are-willing-to-earn-less-money-to-do-more-meaningful-work.
11 Grenville-Cleave, B. et al. 2021. *Creating the World We Want to Live In*. Routledge.
12 Kennon, S., and T. Kasser. 2001. "Goals, Congruence, and Positive Well-Being: New Empirical Support for Humanistic Theories." *Journal of Humanistic Psychology* 41(1): 30–50.
13 Wrzesniewski, A., and J. E. Dutton. 2001. "Crafting a Job: Revisioning Employees as Active Crafters of Their Work." *Academy of Management Review* 26: 179–201.

Chapter 5

Own the Room, Command the Stage

The first time I flew on the company jet, I felt it before I even boarded. That shift in atmosphere. The unspoken hierarchy. The effortless command of the executives who stepped onto the tarmac as if they'd been born into this world of private terminals and seamless itineraries. The aircraft itself was sleek and pristine, a floating boardroom in the sky. The smell of leather seats, the hushed efficiency of the flight crew, the way conversations carried weight even before takeoff. It was a world apart from anything I had known.

I was nervous. More than nervous. I was intimidated. I had never done this before. I called my boss, whispering into my phone, "Are there any rules I need to know? What should I say? What shouldn't I say?" He laughed, reassuring me that it was just another meeting, just at 40,000 feet. But it didn't feel like just another meeting. It felt like stepping into a different level of leadership, one where every move, every word, every moment of silence mattered.

I took my assigned seat, directly across from the CEO. The engines hummed as we lifted off, soaring high above the world, but I was acutely aware of the conversation unfolding at my table. It wasn't just the words spoken. It was the way they spoke them. Concise. Decisive. No wasted movement, no unnecessary explanation. There was an economy to their presence, a certainty that didn't require volume or theatrics to hold weight.

I sat there, absorbing it all. They weren't just leaders because of their titles. They were leaders because of how they carried themselves. And in that moment, I understood something profound:

Leadership presence isn't about how much space you take up. It's about how much certainty you exude.

These leaders didn't demand attention. They simply carried it with them. It was in their measured responses, their ability to pause before speaking, and the way they made direct eye contact without hesitation.

Over the years, I traveled the world with top executives, sitting in boardrooms where billion-dollar decisions were made, watching how they

DOI: 10.4324/9781003627265-6

navigated high-stakes conversations and how they managed their time, their energy, and their influence. I saw firsthand that leadership presence wasn't about talking the most or being the smartest in the room. It was about composure. It was about knowing who you are, what you stand for, and owning your space with quiet confidence.

I learned that the best leaders never rushed. They never scrambled. They projected clarity, even in the face of uncertainty. They mastered the art of the pause, the weight of a well-timed silence. They didn't fill the air with words just to be heard. They spoke only when they had something worth saying. And when they did, people listened.

I realized that presence is not something you are born with. It is something you cultivate.

This chapter is your guide to that cultivation. To learn how to enter any room and own it, not with force, but with conviction. To build the kind of presence that makes people stop and listen, not because you're the loudest, but because you bring something deeper to the table. We'll explore what it really means to project confidence, to balance competence with warmth, and to develop the kind of presence that doesn't just command attention, it earns trust and inspires action.

Understanding Leadership Presence

Leadership presence is often described in intangible terms. Something you recognize when you see it but struggle to define. Some mistake it for charisma, assuming that those with an outgoing personality or natural charm inherently command attention. Others associate it with dominance, believing that power means taking up space, speaking the loudest, or exerting authority. But true leadership presence isn't about being the loudest or the most charismatic. It's about how you make others feel in your presence.

Presence is the ability to project both competence and warmth,[1] to be credible while also being trustworthy and approachable. It's the subtle yet undeniable quality that makes people lean in when you speak, that makes your words land with impact. It's about creating a gravitational pull. Not by demanding attention, but by embodying clarity, composure, and conviction.

Competence is the foundation of leadership. It's your expertise, your depth of knowledge, your ability to execute. But competence alone isn't enough. Without **warmth**, without a sense of empathy, trust, and human connection, you risk being seen as distant, intimidating, or even unapproachable. However, if warmth overpowers competence, you may struggle to establish authority, leaving your leadership presence feeling diluted.

When you master the art of balancing the two, something powerful happens. You become someone people trust. Not just because you know what you're doing, but because they feel seen, heard, and understood in your presence. You become a leader whose words carry weight, not because they are the loudest, but because they resonate.

I remember one executive I worked with, a leader so poised, so composed, that the moment he entered a room, the energy shifted. He never needed to assert dominance, never needed to prove his intelligence. Instead, he led with quiet authority, a calm presence that invited people into conversation rather than demanding compliance. He understood the power of listening and the impact of a well-timed pause. He knew that leadership wasn't about forcing people to pay attention, but about earning their respect through the way he engaged, the way he spoke with clarity, and the way he made others feel valued in his presence.

That's the key to leadership presence. It's not about performance, but how you communicate, how you carry yourself, and how you lead with conviction while staying deeply rooted in authenticity. And knowing when to step forward with confidence and when to create space for others.

Think of the leaders who have inspired you. *What made them memorable? Was it their ability to command attention without raising their voice? Was it their confidence in uncertainty? Their ability to create a space where people felt heard and valued?* These are not coincidences. They are the marks of leadership presence at work.

And the best part? It's something you can cultivate. It's something you can refine, strengthen, and master over time.

As we move forward, we'll explore how to build this presence and how to develop the confidence, clarity, and connection that define truly impactful leaders. Because leadership presence isn't just about commanding a room but shaping the conversations that define the future.

Embodying Confidence as a Leader

There's a difference between speaking and being heard. Between being present and truly owning a room. Some people walk into a space and instantly command attention. Not because they demand it, but because something about them draws people in. They don't rush their words. They don't fill silences with nervous chatter. They move with intention. They own their presence.

High achievers, particularly women and underrepresented groups, often attribute their success to luck rather than skill.[2] But true leadership presence demands the opposite, that is, a steadfast belief in your own credibility and the willingness to own your expertise.

I once coached someone on my team who hesitated in meetings, unsure if she should speak up. Her insights were valuable, but she second-guessed herself. We worked on anchoring her presence, not through louder words or more aggressive stances, but through stillness.

Through breathing before speaking.

Through making eye contact.

Through leaning into the space instead of shrinking away from it. When she finally embraced her own certainty, people started listening. Not because she changed who she was, but because she started owning it.

This is what Lisa Sun's work on *gravitas* underscores.[3] I once attended a workshop led by Lisa, and one of the messages she shared was that leaders with a presence don't need to overpower a room. Instead, they draw people in through quiet confidence, self-belief, and clarity. True gravitas isn't about dominating a space but shaping it. Leaders who develop this quality don't just command attention. They earn respect through intentionality and presence.

Think of the most captivating leaders you've ever met. They don't over-explain. They don't seek approval. Instead, they speak with clarity and certainty, making every word count. They allow silence to work for them rather than against them. When they walk into a room, they don't shrink into the background. They take up space. Not aggressively, but purposefully, as if they **belong.**

The Art of Presence

Great leaders don't just talk. They listen. They aren't just physically in the room, they are fully present. And when they speak, people stop and pay attention. Not because they are the loudest, but because their words carry weight.

Presence is about the energy you bring into a space. It's about whether people feel seen and heard in your presence. It's about how you hold yourself, not only in moments of confidence but also in moments of uncertainty. *Do you fidget when you feel nervous? Do you avoid eye contact when you feel out of your depth? Do you shrink when challenged?*

Real presence is about staying grounded, even when the stakes are high. It's the ability to regulate your emotions, to slow down instead of rushing through discomfort, and to own your space even when you're unsure of the outcome.

Take Aaron, a senior manager at a global tech company. By all external measures, he was successful. He was sharp, articulate, and knowledgeable in his field. But inside, he often felt like an imposter. Meetings felt like battles where he had to prove his worth. When challenged, he spoke quickly, his voice rising slightly, his hands restless on the table. If a senior executive questioned him, he found himself either over-explaining or completely shutting down.

He didn't realize it, but his energy was signaling uncertainty. People sensed it. His team hesitated to approach him for guidance, reading his body language as closed off. Higher-ups, though they valued his technical expertise, weren't convinced he had the leadership presence for the next level. He was caught in a cycle of doubt: the more he struggled to be heard, the more his credibility diminished.

Then came a turning point. Aaron attended a leadership program where, instead of focusing on what to say, he was asked to focus on how he showed up. One exercise required him to sit in silence for two minutes before responding to a challenging question. It was excruciating. His heart pounded. His impulse was to jump in, to prove he had the answer. But he forced himself to breathe, to let the discomfort settle.

When he finally spoke, something shifted. His voice was calmer, slower. His words landed differently. He saw the change in the room. People weren't just hearing him, they were listening.

Aaron began practicing this in real meetings. He trained himself to pause, to hold eye contact, to let a question linger before responding. He became conscious of his breath, ensuring it stayed steady even in moments of tension. He started noticing how leaders he admired carried themselves. They didn't rush or react. They owned their space.

Aaron's transformation was gradual but unmistakable. Six months later, he was presenting a new idea to a team of senior executives. One pushed back hard on his proposal. The old Aaron would have panicked. But this time, he took a slow breath. He held eye contact. Instead of immediately rebutting, he nodded, acknowledging the concern. Then he responded. Not with defensiveness, but with clarity.

The energy in the room shifted. The executive leaned in, listening. His team took note. And for the first time, Aaron felt it: presence. Not just being seen, but felt.

That moment changed everything. His team became more engaged and more willing to seek his guidance. His peers saw him as a leader, not just a technical expert. And when the time came for a promotion discussion, his name was at the top of the list, not because he had learned to say more, but because he had mastered the power of saying less, with presence.

This is what great leaders understand: presence isn't about being the loudest voice in the room. It's about being the most intentional one.

Commanding Attention with Authenticity

Too often, people think commanding a room means performing. Adopting a bigger personality, speaking in a louder voice, and taking up more space than feels natural. But real presence isn't about pretending to be someone you're not. It's about owning who you are, unapologetically.

People follow leaders who are comfortable in their own skin. A leader who walks into a room with forced confidence comes across as inauthentic.

But a leader who speaks with conviction, who is honest about what they know and what they don't, commands attention in a way that feels effortless.

A friend of mine, Isla, had spent most of her career feeling like she had to *perform* to be taken seriously. She was a director at a consulting firm, advising executives on strategy and transformation. In a male-dominated industry, she had been told early on that she needed to be "more assertive," "more commanding," and "more like a CEO."

So she tried. She deepened her voice when she spoke in meetings. She forced herself to use power poses before presentations. She perfected a mask of confidence, even when she was unsure. But something never quite clicked.

Despite doing everything she was supposed to, she still struggled to hold the room. When she spoke, people nodded but didn't seem moved. She left meetings feeling exhausted like she had been acting in a role that wasn't hers.

Then came the breaking point. She was giving a major presentation to the executive team, pitching a bold new strategy. She had spent weeks rehearsing every line, perfecting every slide. But ten minutes in, the CEO cut her off.

"This sounds well-prepared," he said. "But I want to know what *you* think. Not what you think we want to hear. Strip away the script. What's your real take?"

Isla froze. Her pulse quickened. She looked around the room, feeling exposed. But instead of scrambling to reframe her answer in executive-speak, she did something different. She let go of the performance.

And then she spoke.

She dropped the rehearsed phrases. She stopped worrying about sounding like a leader and just spoke like herself: direct, thoughtful, and deeply insightful.

The energy in the room shifted. The CEO leaned forward. Her colleagues stopped checking their phones. For the first time, they weren't just hearing her words. They were listening to her.

That moment changed how Isla showed up. She stopped forcing herself to be louder. Instead, she leaned into what made her *her* – her ability to synthesize complex ideas, her quiet conviction, and her willingness to admit when she was still working through a challenge.

Over the next year, people began coming to her not just for expertise but for perspective. Clients requested her by name. A senior leader pulled her aside after a meeting and said, "I don't know what changed, but you've got something different now. When you talk, people pay attention."

It wasn't magic. It was authenticity.

Because confidence isn't about knowing everything. It's about trusting yourself enough to navigate the unknown.

Mastering Storytelling for Influence

Facts inform. But stories? Stories inspire.

The best leaders don't just present data. They tell stories. They use narratives to make their message stick, to create an emotional connection, and to move people toward action.

Storytelling is a powerful tool for persuasion. It activates more areas of the brain than logic alone, making messages more memorable and engaging. A well-told story can turn a simple idea into a movement.

Think about the leaders who have impacted you most. Chances are, they didn't just tell you what to do. They showed you why it mattered through the power of story.

Great storytelling in leadership isn't about making things up, but finding the human moments that bring ideas to life. Sharing challenges, struggles, and lessons in a way that resonates with the people listening.

When Evan took over as VP of Operations at a mid-sized manufacturing company, he had one major challenge: safety compliance was abysmal. Incident rates were climbing, audits flagged repeated issues, and frontline workers treated safety briefings as an afterthought.

So he did what most leaders would do. He laid out the facts.

He showed charts. He ran training sessions. He sent emails packed with statistics about how small mistakes led to serious injuries. But nothing changed. Workers still rushed through procedures. Supervisors still cut corners to meet deadlines. The message wasn't landing.

Then, one day, something shifted.

At the start of a routine all-hands meeting, Evan put the slides away. Instead, he pulled up a picture of an older man, standing beside a teenage boy at a baseball game. The man had a prosthetic leg.

"I want to tell you about Tom," Evan said, his voice steady but full of weight. "Tom worked in a plant just like this one. He was one of the best operators on the floor. Knew every process inside and out. He was a mentor to dozens of new hires."

He paused, scanning the room. The usual murmur of side conversations was gone. People were listening.

"One day, Tom was in a hurry. He skipped a lockout procedure – just this once, just to save a few minutes."

Evan exhaled, looking at the photo again.

"That mistake cost him his leg. And it changed his life."

He pointed to the teenager.

"That's his son. Tom used to coach his baseball team. He can't run the bases with him anymore. He told me that's what he regrets the most – not the pain, not the surgeries. But missing out on those moments."

The room was silent.

"Safety isn't about rules. It's about lives. It's about families. It's about making sure *you* get to be there for the things that matter."

From that day on, safety meetings were different. People started taking protocols seriously. Not because they were afraid of penalties, but because they understood what was at stake. Supervisors stopped skipping steps. Operators began looking out for each other. Evan's message finally landed.

Not because of data. Not because of rules.

Because of a story.

That's the power of storytelling in leadership. It transforms dry information into something that people feel. It turns compliance into commitment. It makes messages stick. A leader who masters storytelling doesn't just communicate. They create change.

Turning Presence into Influence

Leadership presence isn't about taking up space. It's about transforming it. The confidence people gain from your leadership. The trust they build in your vision. The way your words don't just fade into the background but *stick:* shaping perspectives, shifting mindsets, and sparking action.

When you cultivate true leadership presence, you don't just own the room.

You *move* the people in it.

But presence alone isn't enough.

Because leadership isn't just about being seen. It's about *influence:* the ability to shape decisions, drive action, and create lasting impact.

And influence? That's the new currency of leadership.

In the next chapter, we'll explore why influence is at the core of modern leadership and how those who master it hold the key to unlocking change.

Notes

1 Cuddy, A. 2018. *Presence: Bringing Your Boldest Self to Your Biggest Challenges*. Little, Brown and Company.
2 Young, V. 2011. *The Secret Thoughts of Successful Women: And Men: Why Capable People Suffer from Impostor Syndrome and How to Thrive in Spite of It*. Crown Currency.
3 Sun, L. 2023. *Gravitas: The 8 Strengths That Redefine Confidence*. Hay House.

Chapter 6

Influence Is the New Currency

The first time I saw real influence at play, it wasn't in a boardroom. It wasn't during a high-stakes negotiation or a keynote speech. It was on my phone.

A single post. A few lines of text. A carefully framed video. Within hours, tens of thousands of people were engaging, debating, and sharing. The person behind it wasn't a CEO, a politician, or a Fortune 500 executive. But they *had* mastered the modern art of influence. Someone who understood that in today's world, power doesn't just come from authority. It comes from attention.

We are living in a world where influence is currency, where a well-placed message can shape narratives faster than a press release. A single voice, amplified correctly, can disrupt industries, challenge norms, and create movements.

But influence isn't about going viral. You don't need to have the loudest voice or the biggest following. Influence comes from something else.

It's the ability to build trust so that when you speak, people believe you.

It's the ability to foster collaboration so that when you lead, people follow.

It's the ability to inspire action so that when you step into a room, the energy shifts.

I've sat at tables with executives who held immense power but struggled to rally commitment from their team. And I've seen others, often with no formal authority, shape decisions and shift perspectives simply by how they showed up, how they connected, and how they earned the right to be heard.

The difference? *Trust. Presence. Credibility.*

In this chapter, we'll break down the mechanics of influence and discuss how to cultivate trust, shape conversations that drive action, and use influence to create real, lasting change. Because leadership isn't just about holding a title. It's about earning the right to be heard. And in a world

DOI: 10.4324/9781003627265-7

where influence moves faster than ever, those who master it hold the key to the future.

The Foundation of Influence: Why It Matters

In today's world, where traditional command and control leadership is rapidly fading, influence has become the most valuable leadership skill. Authority alone no longer guarantees followership. Titles don't automatically earn trust.

The most effective leaders aren't the ones who dictate. They're the ones who persuade, align, and inspire – who move people toward a shared goal.

The Art and Science of Influence

A lot has been written about leadership, especially related to the new future of work.[1] [2] [3] [4] [5] Leaders who can influence across all levels of an organization, whether it be peers, executives, frontline teams, or external stakeholders, are the ones who drive real change.

They don't rely on authority. They build alignment.

They don't push. They create momentum.

And when influence is wielded with integrity, it doesn't just advance individual careers, it fuels progress that benefits entire organizations.

Dr. Robert Cialdini,[6] one of the leading experts on influence, defines this as the ability to create alignment with people's needs, beliefs, and values. His six principles of influence, reciprocity, commitment and consistency, social proof, authority, liking, and scarcity, offer a framework for understanding how humans make decisions.

- **Reciprocity:** People feel compelled to return favors and gestures. Leaders who give first, who offer support, insight, or mentorship without expectation, build relationships that make others more likely to engage, trust, and support them in return.
- **Commitment and Consistency:** Humans crave alignment between their beliefs and actions. When leaders help people articulate a commitment, whether to a goal, a value, or a vision, they create a natural pull toward follow-through.
- **Social Proof:** We look to others for cues on how to behave. A leader who can highlight widespread buy-in, "This approach has already driven success for teams just like ours," makes action feel not just possible, but inevitable.
- **Authority:** We trust those who demonstrate expertise. But authority today isn't just about credentials. It's about credibility. Leaders who

consistently add value and who prove their competence through action naturally command attention.

- **Liking:** People are more easily persuaded by those they like and relate to. Leadership isn't about being everyone's best friend, but it is about building genuine rapport. People follow those they feel connected to.
- **Scarcity:** We assign a higher value to things that feel rare or time-sensitive. Leaders who can articulate *why now* – why this decision, this initiative, this moment create urgency that moves people to act.

Frameworks for Influence and Change

At its core, influence is about aligning others' perspectives and motivations with your vision. In this section, I'll share three frameworks that can help you influence others and drive change: Kotter's 8-Step Change Model, Self-Determination Theory (SDT), and The Heath Brothers' Model for Change.

Kotter's 8-Step Change Model

Influence isn't just about getting people to say *yes*. It's about getting them to *believe* in the change, to champion it as if it were their own. And that happens through emotion, momentum, and meaningful action. That's why sustainable change requires more than just a plan.

Dr. John Kotter's *8-Step Change Model*[7] [8] provides a roadmap for turning influence into action, guiding leaders through the process of introducing change and making it *stick*. The model underscores something critical: change is a social and emotional exercise. People don't just need to *understand* the need for change. They need to *feel* it.

The steps are simple in concept but powerful in execution:

1 **Create a Sense of Urgency:** Show people why change must happen *now*.
2 **Build a Guiding Coalition:** Bring together a group of influential individuals to drive the change.
3 **Form a Strategic Vision and Initiatives:** Define a clear picture of success and how to get there.
4 **Enlist a Volunteer Army:** Get people invested in making the change happen.
5 **Enable Action by Removing Barriers:** Break down obstacles that prevent progress.
6 **Generate Short-Term Wins:** Deliver quick, visible successes to maintain momentum.

7 **Sustain Acceleration:** Keep pushing forward by building on early successes.
8 **Institute Change:** Embed the new way of working into the culture, making it the norm.

Now, let's explore how these elements played out in a real-world example.

The Global System That Transformed a Company

The first leadership meeting on the global information system felt like déjà vu. Around the table sat executives from different regions, each carrying years of frustration. The conversation played out the way it always had. Reports took too long. Data was unreliable. Leadership lacked visibility into performance. Acquired businesses operated with different systems, processes, and ways of doing things.

The frustration was understandable. The parent company wanted real-time access to global performance metrics, but the reality was a mess of manual reports, disconnected spreadsheets, and outdated processes. Decisions weren't being made proactively because leaders didn't have the right data at the right time.

Silence settled over the room after the usual grievances had been aired. No one had faith in another system rollout. They had seen it all before. Big promises, complex implementations, minimal results.

But what struck me most wasn't the technical failures. It was the human ones. Finance teams scrambling at month-end, manually pulling numbers from different sources just to give leadership a report they still didn't trust. Regional managers making gut decisions because they didn't have timely insights. Frontline teams caught between outdated tools and increasing pressure to deliver results.

This wasn't just an issue of efficiency. It was an issue of trust. And no one follows a leader who walks in with sweeping promises of transformation. They had seen that before. They had learned not to believe it.

So, I didn't start with a plan. I started with a story.

Step 1: Create a Sense of Urgency

The first conversation wasn't about system upgrades or automation. It was about what happens when businesses operate in the dark.

A factory leader had flagged a potential issue in one of our key production lines. But instead of diagnosing the problem immediately, teams had to pull data from five different systems – none of which spoke to each other.

Step 2: Build a Guiding Coalition

This problem wasn't going to be solved by a company policy. Real change needed real buy-in.

The usual top-down approach wouldn't work, so I looked elsewhere. Who actually felt the pain of this system every day? Who had the most at stake?

- A regional operations lead who had spent years fighting with outdated tools just to get basic insights.
- A finance leader who had lived through the nightmare of manual month-end reporting.
- A technology partner who understood the complexity of integrating different systems across multiple acquired businesses.

Together, we built a coalition. It wasn't a formal steering committee burdened by bureaucracy but a group of people who knew exactly what wasn't working and had ideas about how to fix it.

I didn't ask them for feedback. I asked them: *If you could rebuild how data flows in this company, what would you change?*

Suddenly, people weren't just talking about problems. They were designing solutions.

Step 3: Form a Strategic Vision and Initiatives

With the right people aligned, the vision became clear:

Empower the business with real-time, accurate, and accessible data to drive better decisions.

This wasn't a vague mission statement. It was backed by clear, practical initiatives:

- Automate manual reporting so finance and operations teams can focus on strategy, not spreadsheets.
- Integrate data across all acquired businesses, creating a single source of truth.
- Ensure accessibility so leaders can pull performance insights without waiting for reports to be compiled.

For the first time, this project wasn't an abstract IT investment. It was a business transformation that people could see themselves in.

Step 4: Enlist a Volunteer Army

This transformation wasn't going to happen because leadership demanded it. It needed people on the ground to champion the change.

So instead of pushing adoption through mandates, I put out a call: *If you want to be part of fixing this, let's do it together.*

People showed up. Not because they were required to but because they had spent years dealing with these inefficiencies firsthand. The project was no longer being forced on them. It was something they were building themselves.

When people see their fingerprints on a solution, they fight for it.

Step 5: Enable Action by Removing Barriers

Ideas weren't the problem. Approval processes were.

The existing system for implementing process changes was slow, bureaucratic, and frustrating. Nothing moved forward without layers of sign-off, and by the time approvals came through, the business had already moved on.

So, we flipped the model.

- Any team could test a system integration within 30 days if it improved efficiency and had cross-functional support.
- Pilots didn't require corporate sign-off, only validation from those who would use them.
- Standardized reporting dashboards replaced complex, manual processes.

The goal wasn't to create another system people had to *adapt* to. The goal was to build a system *that worked for them.*

Step 6: Generate Short-Term Wins

Within two months, reports that previously took two weeks to compile were available in minutes.

Within four months, leadership had real-time access to global performance metrics, eliminating the need for last-minute data scrambles.

This wasn't a massive overhaul overnight. These were small, visible wins and proof that the change was working.

Step 7: Sustain Acceleration

The initial success was critical, but momentum fades if people feel like change is temporary. Sustaining progress required two things:

- Real-time feedback loops: Monthly debriefs allowed teams to continuously refine the system, ensuring it worked *for* them, not *against* them.
- Recognition beyond success: Effort mattered as much as results. If a team tested a process change and it didn't work, there was no punishment, only learning.

People kept innovating because they weren't afraid to fail.

Step 8: Institute Change

One year later, this wasn't just a new system, it was a new way of working.

Reports weren't a bottleneck. Leadership had real-time access to global data. Teams no longer relied on guesswork.

But more than that, a cultural shift had taken root. New employees didn't step into a fragmented system. They stepped into a company where data-driven decision-making was the norm and not the exception.

Self-Determination Theory

Compliance might get people to follow a directive, but real commitment, which sustains transformation, comes from something different. It comes from within.

This is the foundation of *Self-Determination Theory*, developed by psychologists Edward Deci and Richard Ryan.[9] [10] [11] Their research revealed that the most powerful motivators aren't external rewards or punishments but the *intrinsic* drivers that shape human behavior. When people feel a sense of ownership over their choices, confidence in their abilities, and a meaningful connection to others, they are *naturally* motivated to grow, adapt, and perform at their best.

SDT identifies three fundamental psychological needs that fuel this internal drive: autonomy, competence, and relatedness. When leaders understand and apply these principles, people *choose* it for themselves. But theories alone don't create an impact. It's the way they play out in real life that makes the difference.

A Software Engineer Who Rebuilt the Culture

When Sofia was promoted to lead a software development team, she thought she had the perfect setup. She inherited a team of incredibly talented engineers, some of the best in their field. The company invested heavily in innovation, and the leadership team had high expectations for breakthroughs.

But something was off.

Deadlines were being missed. Brainstorming sessions felt forced, like no one wanted to speak up. Some of the best engineers were disengaging: doing the bare minimum, clocking out when their work was done.

Sofia ran the numbers. Productivity was low. Turnover was climbing. A few engineers had already moved to competitors, and others were quietly looking for exits.

She needed to turn things around. Fast.

At first, she did what most leaders would do. She offered incentives. More bonuses. More public recognition. More perks.

None of it worked.

That's when she came across SDT. It made her rethink everything. The real problem wasn't a lack of compensation or external rewards. It was a lack of *intrinsic motivation*. The engineers didn't feel like they had control over their work. They didn't feel like they were growing. And they didn't feel truly connected to the team.

So, she stopped trying to *motivate* them from the outside. Instead, she focused on *creating an environment where motivation could thrive from within*.

Step 1: Autonomy – Giving Control Back to the Experts

Sofia realized that most engineers felt they had no say in their work. Project roadmaps were dictated from the top down. Innovation was expected, but there was no room to experiment outside rigid structures.

She changed that.

Instead of prescribing how work should be done, she gave the team the freedom to decide. She created "innovation windows," which were blocks of time where engineers could work on passion projects, experiment with new ideas, and explore solutions that *they* believed in.

The shift was immediate. Engineers who had been disengaged started bringing new ideas to meetings. Some of their projects, initially just side experiments, became core features in the company's products.

Autonomy wasn't about *stepping back*. It was about *empowering* people to own their work. And once they felt that ownership, they didn't just meet expectations, they *exceeded* them.

Step 2: Competence – Making Growth Inevitable

The next issue was confidence. Some of the engineers were struggling with imposter syndrome. They felt like they were falling behind. The fear of failure made them hesitant to take risks.

So, Sofia didn't just tell them they were capable, she made sure they *felt* it.

She invested in mentorship programs, pairing senior engineers with junior team members for collaborative learning. She brought in guest speakers from the industry to share insights, not just on technical skills but on *how to stay ahead in a field that was constantly changing*.

She also made it safe to fail.

In team meetings, she started celebrating *learning moments*. Not just wins, but risks taken, experiments attempted, and lessons learned. The message was clear: failure wasn't a setback. Actually, it was part of the process.

Slowly, the hesitation faded. Engineers started speaking up, pushing boundaries, and testing ideas they once held back. Their confidence grew. And as it did, so did the team's momentum.

Step 3: Relatedness – Building a Team That Actually Felt Like One

The final and perhaps most important shift was how the team connected.

Despite working together for years, there was little genuine *camaraderie*. Meetings were transactional. Slack messages were all about logistics. There was no *team culture*.

Sofia changed that, too.

She started hosting informal gatherings, some virtual, some in person, where work wasn't the main topic. She initiated a "Pair & Share" program, where team members were randomly matched each week for casual one-on-one conversations.

Then, she made one bold move that changed everything.

She asked every engineer to share a personal story. Their journey into tech, the obstacles they had overcome, and what made them stay in the industry.

At first, people were hesitant. But as the stories came out, so did a realization: behind the algorithms and the code, they were *humans first*.

From that point on, collaboration wasn't just about efficiency. It was about *supporting* each other. Engineers who had once worked in silos started offering help before it was asked. Tough conversations became easier. The walls between them, some invisible, some built over years of corporate structure, began to fall.

And with that, the final piece of intrinsic motivation clicked into place.

The Impact of Intrinsic Motivation

Within months, everything changed.

Deadlines were being met, not because of pressure but because the team was *driven* to succeed. Productivity soared. Engineers who had once planned to leave decided to stay.

By the end of the year, the team had launched one of the most successful products in the company's history. It wasn't just a technical achievement. It was proof that people *want* to do great work when they are given the freedom, support, and connection to make it happen.

Sofia hadn't forced the team to change.

She had simply created the *conditions* where change became inevitable.

The Heath Brothers' Model for Change

Logic alone doesn't move people. Neither does emotion on its own. Real change, the kind that sticks, requires both.

Chip and Dan Heath, in their book *Switch: How to Change Things When Change is Hard,*[12] use a simple metaphor to explain why change so often fails: inside every person, there is a *Rider* and an *Elephant.*

The Rider represents the rational mind, the part of us that analyzes, strategizes, and plans. The Elephant is the emotional side: the force of habits, fears, desires, and deeply held values.

The problem? The Rider can see the way forward, but without motivation, the Elephant won't move. The Elephant can charge ahead, but without direction, it gets lost. If a leader doesn't guide both, change stalls before it even begins.

And yet, when both are aligned, transformation happens. People don't just understand the change; they *feel* it. And they act on it.

But theory only matters if it works in real life. Let's look at how a leader applied this model to turn around an organization stuck in uncertainty.

A CEO Who Turned a Failing Merger into a Movement

When Hannah was appointed CEO of a global logistics company, she walked into a storm.

The company had recently merged with a competitor, creating what should have been an industry powerhouse. But inside, things were falling apart. Employees from both organizations were clashing. Leadership teams were struggling to integrate. The merger, instead of creating momentum, had stalled progress.

Departments operated in silos, reluctant to share knowledge. Longtime employees felt like their expertise was being discarded. The newly acquired workforce felt like outsiders. And clients, once loyal, were starting to lose trust.

The logical steps had been taken. Financial models had been run. Organizational charts had been updated. Policies had been rewritten. The *Rider* had been given all the instructions it needed.

But the *Elephant,* the emotions, the fear, and the identity struggles, was being ignored.

Hannah knew that the company would crumble under its own weight if she didn't get people to want this change.

So, she used the Heath Brothers' model to move the organization forward.

Step 1: Direct the Rider – Making Change Clear and Doable

The first problem was complexity. Employees felt like they were drowning in uncertainty: unsure of roles, responsibilities, and what the merger *meant* for them.

Hannah knew she had to make the change concrete.

She didn't roll out another vague "integration strategy." Instead, she defined three *clear, specific* priorities:

1. Every department would have a shared, unified process within 90 days.
2. Cross-functional teams would be assigned to tackle customer retention immediately.
3. All leaders at every level would hold open town halls to answer questions.

No long-winded transformation plans. No overwhelming change initiatives. Just *three things:* tangible, achievable, and easy to rally behind.

For the first time, people could see the road ahead.

Step 2: Motivate the Elephant – Making Change Feel Personal

But clarity wasn't enough. The resistance wasn't logical. It was *emotional.* People were grieving the loss of their old company culture. Longtime employees felt sidelined. New employees felt like intruders. The Elephant was digging in its heels.

So Hannah stopped talking about corporate strategy and started talking about *people.*

She met with frontline employees. She listened to their frustrations. And then she told a different kind of story.

She stood before her team and talked about her father, who had spent his entire career in the shipping industry. She spoke about how, when she was a child, she used to sit on the floor of his office as he ran operations for a small logistics firm. How she had watched him build relationships with clients, not just as customers but as *partners.* How she learned, early on, that this industry wasn't just about moving goods. It was about *trust.*

And then she said this:

"We didn't merge two companies. We merged two histories. And if we do this right, we won't just be a bigger company. We'll be a *better* one. One where your expertise still matters. One where the legacy you built doesn't disappear, it evolves."

For the first time, people *felt* the meaning of the merger. It wasn't about loss. It was about *building something new together.*

The mood shifted.

Leaders started having different conversations with their teams. Employees began seeing colleagues from the other side of the merger not as competitors but as part of a shared future.

The Elephant was starting to move.

Step 3: Shape the Path – Removing Barriers to Make Change Easy

Even with motivation, Hannah knew that if the day-to-day environment made change difficult, people would return to old habits.

So she made change easy.

She eliminated outdated policies that created unnecessary divisions between the two merged companies. She created mixed teams, forcing collaboration, but in a way that felt natural, not forced. And she made sure leaders at all levels were rewarded not for protecting their turf but for *building bridges*.

She also tackled one of the biggest sources of tension: recognition.

Before, employees from the acquired company felt like outsiders, like their contributions weren't valued. So Hannah reshaped how success was celebrated. At every all-hands meeting, she highlighted stories of cross-company collaboration, publicly recognizing individuals who had made the merger *work*.

The barriers weren't just operational. They were *emotional*. And by shaping the path, she cleared them.

The Moment It All Changed

Six months into the merger, something happened that told Hannah the shift was real.

A senior manager, one of the loudest skeptics of the merger, stood up at a leadership meeting and said, "I'll be honest. I didn't think this was going to work. I thought we would spend years fighting over who did things better. But last week, I was on a call with a team that didn't exist before this merger – three from our side and three from theirs. And we solved a problem in *half* the time it would have taken us before. I don't just see the value in this now. I *feel* it."

That was it. The moment the culture truly shifted.

The merger stopped being something that happened *to* them. It became something *they* were part of.

And when the numbers came in at the end of the year, it was clear: revenue was up, employee engagement had increased, and customer retention had stabilized.

Not because of more rules. Not because of top-down enforcement. But because the people *inside* the company had decided, for themselves, to embrace the change.

Building Trust as the Foundation of Influence

The leaders who shape industries, transform organizations, and move people toward meaningful change aren't the ones with the loudest voices or the most polished strategies. They are the ones who have earned the right to be heard, who have built trust so deeply that when they speak, people *listen*. Not out of obligation, but out of belief.

Dr. Paul Zak's research[13] confirms what great leaders have always known: high-trust environments drive higher productivity, engagement, and innovation. When people trust their leaders, they don't just comply with change, and they *embrace* it. They take risks, share ideas, and invest in the vision, not because they have to, but because they *want* to.

But trust isn't given freely. It's built. And it's built through the small, everyday moments of leadership: reliability, openness, and empathy.

Let's explore what that looks like in practice.

The CFO Who Changed the Culture with Trust

When Ethan was promoted to Chief Financial Officer CFO) of a local manufacturing company, he quickly realized he had inherited more than spreadsheets and budgets. He had inherited a *trust problem*.

For years, the finance department had been seen as the company's enforcer: the place where ideas went to die. Leaders from other departments resented finance, believing it operated in a vacuum, making decisions without understanding the impact on actual operations.

The culture was one of defensiveness. Business unit leaders held back information, fearing it would be used against them. Teams worked in silos, reluctant to collaborate. And innovation? It had all but disappeared.

Ethan knew that no amount of financial restructuring, strategic planning, or efficiency initiatives would change the company unless he changed *this*.

And that meant rebuilding trust.

Step 1: Reliability – Doing What You Say, Every Time

Ethan's first step wasn't to issue a grand statement about transformation. It was to make a simple promise.

He met with department heads and told them this:

"Finance will no longer be a roadblock. We will be your partner. But partnership requires honesty on both sides. I will commit to full transparency in how decisions are made. In return, I need the same from you."

And then he followed through.

When a product development team submitted a funding request, expecting the usual rejection, Ethan did something different. Instead of shutting it down with a spreadsheet, he walked into their workspace, sat with the engineers, and asked them to *explain* their vision. He listened not just to the numbers but to the *why* behind them.

The request still needed adjustments, but instead of a flat refusal, Ethan worked *with* the team to find a solution. The funding was approved with conditions they could all agree on.

Word spread fast.

For the first time in years, finance wasn't seen as an obstacle. It was seen as a *partner*. And because Ethan followed through on his promise, leaders across the company started bringing finance into discussions *before* problems arose instead of hiding issues until they became crises.

Step 2: Openness – Bringing Transparency into the Conversation

Trust dies in secrecy. If people think decisions are being made behind closed doors, they disengage.

Ethan knew this was a problem. The finance team had historically operated in isolation, presenting budgets and directives with no real explanation of the reasoning behind them. That had to change.

So he took a radical approach: he made the company's financial data more *accessible*.

He started hosting open financial briefings. Meetings where employees from any department could come and ask questions about the company's financial health, investment strategies, and budget priorities. No sugarcoating. No vague responses. Just honest transparency.

At first, employees were skeptical. They had never been invited into these conversations before. But over time, something shifted.

People started *trusting* the numbers because they *understood* them.

They stopped seeing finance as an adversary and started seeing it as a resource. Leaders in product, sales, and operations began making better decisions. Not because they were forced to, but because they finally knew how their work impacted the company's overall success.

Trust grew, not because Ethan *demanded* it but because he *earned* it through transparency.

Step 3: Empathy – Seeing the People, Not Just the Problems

The biggest shift came when Ethan made an unexpected move.

He asked to shadow frontline workers.

Not for a Public Relations (PR) stunt. Not for a leadership exercise. But because he genuinely wanted to *understand* how financial decisions affected the people doing the work.

For two weeks, he spent time on the factory floor, in the warehouses, and in sales meetings. He saw firsthand how budget cuts had impacted staffing. He listened to employees talk about how outdated systems were slowing them down. He sat with customer service reps who fielded complaints from frustrated clients and heard how financial constraints had made it harder to resolve issues.

Then, he did something even more surprising.

At the next executive meeting, instead of leading with numbers, he led with *stories*. He shared what he had seen, what he had heard, and what he had *felt*.

It changed everything.

Suddenly, finance wasn't just about cost-cutting. It was about *people*. Conversations shifted from "What can we afford?" to "What will have the biggest impact?"

The finance team itself changed, too. They started spending more time in the field, engaging with employees at all levels. Decision-making became more collaborative. And when hard financial choices had to be made, people trusted that they were being made *with* them, not *against* them.

The Impact of Trust

A year later, the results spoke for themselves.

Productivity had increased. Cross-departmental collaboration was at an all-time high. Employee engagement scores, once dangerously low, had improved significantly.

And innovation, which had been stagnant for years, was thriving. Teams were experimenting again. Leaders were willing to take risks.

Not because they had been forced to. But because they finally *trusted* the system they were working in.

Ethan hadn't imposed authority. He had built *influence*.

And that influence had transformed not just how decisions were made but how people *felt* about the work they were doing.

Practical Strategies for Cultivating Influence

Now that we've explored the foundations of influence, trust, and motivation, let's turn to *action*. How do you take these principles and make them work in real-world situations? Let's explore what that looks like in practice.

Create Alignment with Shared Values

People don't resist change itself. They resist change that feels misaligned with their values. A leader's most powerful tool is the ability to show people that change isn't about taking something *away* from them but about reinforcing what they already believe in.

When Michael took over as plant manager at a long-established manufacturing facility, he had one major challenge: getting buy-in for automation. His workforce, many of whom had been with the company for decades, saw the shift as a direct threat to their jobs.

He could have tried to convince them with efficiency metrics and cost savings. But that wouldn't have worked.

Instead, he asked them what they valued most. Their answer was immediate: *job security and craftsmanship.*

So he reframed the change. Automation, he told them, wasn't about replacing workers. It was about removing *the most repetitive, dangerous tasks* so they could focus on the skilled, high-value work that made their company stand out. He showed them examples of other plants that had implemented automation without layoffs. He invited workers to help shape how the new processes would integrate with existing expertise.

And slowly, resistance faded. Because it wasn't about forcing a new system, it was about protecting what they already valued.

Change doesn't happen when people are forced into it. It happens when they see it as an extension of what matters most to them.

Use Reciprocity to Build Stronger Relationships

Robert Cialdini's research on reciprocity shows that when people receive something – help, support, recognition – they feel an innate desire to give something back. However, in leadership, reciprocity isn't about *owing* someone a favor. It's about creating a culture of trust, where people naturally *want* to support each other.

Samantha, a senior project manager at an aerospace firm, had a problem. She needed cross-functional teams to work together on a tight deadline. The problem? They didn't report to her. And they had their own priorities.

She could have demanded that the teams work together, a mandate of sorts. Instead, she started by offering help. She anticipated challenges each team might face and connected them with resources, and advocated for extra funding that made their workloads easier. She acknowledged their expertise and asked for their insights.

So when she needed their buy-in, they gave it willingly – because they trusted that she wasn't just there to take, she was there to contribute.

The most influential leaders don't *ask* for support first. They *give* first.

Leverage Social Proof for Change Adoption

When people feel uncertain, they look to others for cues on how to act.

But, the best way isn't to *tell* people what to do. It's to *show* them that others are already doing it.

When the leadership team at a global energy company decided to shift toward renewable initiatives, they faced internal skepticism. Employees were used to the traditional oil and gas model. Many doubted whether renewables could be a profitable focus.

Instead of mandating belief, the CEO leveraged social proof. He didn't just talk about strategy. He shared case studies of competitors who have already made the shift successfully and highlighted internal teams who had piloted small renewable projects. He asked respected company veterans to speak about why they believed this was the future.

The message was clear: *this isn't theory. It's happening. And people you trust are leading the way.* And when people see others like them succeeding, change stops feeling like a risk and starts feeling like *the norm.*

Appeal to Both Logic and Emotion

Most leaders instinctively rely on facts, figures, and analysis to drive decisions. But logic alone rarely moves people. The best communicators know how to engage both the mind *and* the heart. We talk about leading with the heart in Chapter 9.

When Alan, a supply chain executive, needed to convince his team to overhaul their logistics network, he had the data. He could show, in black and white, how inefficient their current system was. How much money they were losing. How much smoother operations could be.

But he didn't start with a spreadsheet.

He started with a story about a small business, one of their longtime customers, who had nearly lost their contract because of delays in product delivery. He described the impact on their employees, their reputation, and their ability to survive.

Then, and only then, did he present the numbers.

When he finished speaking, the team wasn't just on board. They *wanted* to fix the problem.

Data informs. Stories inspire. The best leaders use both.

Create a Sense of Urgency

John Kotter's research on change leadership shows that urgency isn't about panic, but making the *need* for change impossible to ignore.

When Elise, the COO of a financial services firm, saw a new fintech competitor gaining traction, she knew her company had to modernize.

Fast. But her leadership team was dragging their feet. They saw no reason to disrupt their comfortable, familiar ways of working.

So she changed the conversation.

She walked into the next executive meeting, pulled up a live feed of their competitor's website, and showed how many new customers had signed up that *week*. Then, she showed their own declining retention rate.

The message was clear: *We don't have time to wait.*

Urgency isn't about fear. It's about helping people see that *now* is the only time that matters.

Empower Others to Own the Change

People are more likely to commit to change when they *feel they've had a role in shaping it.* That's why the most effective leaders don't dictate every step. They invite people into the process.

When Jordan, an executive at a global consumer goods company, needed to revamp their sustainability efforts, he didn't hand down an edict. He asked employees to submit ideas on how to make operations greener.

The result? Hundreds of creative, practical solutions. And when they implemented the best ones, those employees became the loudest champions of the change because they had helped create it.

Change doesn't stick when people feel it's being done *to* them. It sticks when they feel like they're doing it *with* you.

Influence as the Foundation for Transformational Leadership

The most impactful leaders recognize that influence is not about control but about creating the right conditions for others to step into their own power, contribute meaningfully, and drive progress forward together.

Trust, credibility, and alignment sustain influence over time. When you connect individual motivations with collective goals, teams no longer see change as something imposed from above. A shift occurs, and people embrace transformation as their own, fostering movements that outlast a single leader or initiative. Influence becomes a foundation for meaningful, purpose-driven leadership.

Next, let's turn our focus to innovation as a critical step in ensuring that influence drives real, lasting progress. Leaders who embrace new ways of thinking, encourage bold problem-solving, and remove barriers to creativity are the ones who shape the future. Influence may open the door, but innovation ensures the journey leads somewhere extraordinary.

Notes

1 Geerts, J. M. 2024. "Maximizing the Impact and ROI of Leadership Development: A Theory- and Evidence-informed Framework." *Behavioral Sciences* 14(10): 955. https://doi.org/10.3390/bs14100955.

2 Abu Orabi, T., M. S. Almasarweh, M. K. Qteishat, H. A. Qudah, and M. Z. AlQudah. 2024. "Mapping Leadership and Organizational Commitment Trends: A Bibliometric Review." *Administrative Sciences* 14(8): 171. https://doi.org/10.3390/admsci14080171.

3 Mendenhall, M. E., J. S. Osland, A. Bird, G. R. Oddou, and M. L. Maznevski (Eds.). 2020. *Research Handbook of Global Leadership: Making a Difference.* Edward Elgar Publishing.

4 Haslam, S. A., S. D. Reicher, and M. J. Platow. 2020. *The New Psychology of Leadership: Identity, Influence, and Power* (2nd ed.). Psychology Press.

5 Harvard Business Publishing. 2023. *Leadership Reframed for the Workplace of the Future*. https://www.harvardbusiness.org/insights/leadership-reframed-for-the-workplace-of-the-future/.

6 Cialdini, R. B. 2021. *Influence: The Psychology of Persuasion* (Revised ed.). HarperCollins Publishers.

7 Kotter, J. P. 2012. *Leading Change*. Harvard Business School Press.

8 Kotter, J. P., V. Akhtar, and G. Gupta. 2021. *Change: How Organizations Achieve Hard-to-Imagine Results in Uncertain and Volatile Times*. Wiley.

9 Ryan, R. M., and E. L. Deci. 2000. "Self-determination Theory and the Facilitation of Intrinsic Motivation, Social Development, and Well-being." *American Psychologist* 55(1): 68–78. https://doi.org/10.1037/0003-066X.55.1.68.

10 Ryan, R. M., and E. L Deci. 2017. *Self-Determination Theory: Basic Psychological Needs in Motivation, Development, and Wellness*. The Guilford Press.

11 Deci, E. L., and R. M. Ryan. 2000. "The "What" and "Why" of Goal Pursuits: Human Needs and the Self-Determination of Behavior." *Psychological Inquiry* 11(4): 227–268. https://doi.org/10.1207/S15327965PLI1104_01.

12 Heath, C., and D. Heath. 2010. *Switch: How to Change Things When Change Is Hard*. Crown Business.

13 Zak, P. J. 2023. *Trust Factor: The Science of Creating High-Performance Companies*. HarperCollins Leadership.

Chapter 7

Spark Ideas, Watch Them Fly

"That's a nice idea, but let's be realistic here."

I heard it time and time again. Not as an outright rejection, but as a subtle reminder to stay in my lane. It came from my colleagues, my bosses, and even that little voice in my head whispering that I should stop pushing so hard. Stop questioning, and challenging. Best to keep your curiosity in check.

But I couldn't do it. I've never been able to. I didn't build global strategies or lead teams at the highest level by playing it safe. I certainly didn't end up as a named inventor on a patent[1] by following the rules. And the best ideas I've ever been part of? They didn't come from someone waiting for permission. They came from a relentless pursuit of what *could be*.

The world has enough rule followers. It needs more thinkers. More questioners. More people willing to push at the edges of what's possible. Not recklessly, but with a deep, unshakable curiosity.

That's what this chapter is about.

Innovation doesn't happen in meeting rooms filled with people who nod along. It happens in spaces where questions are met with enthusiasm, where experiments aren't just tolerated but celebrated. Where the words *What if?* carry more weight than *We've always done it this way*.

The most successful leaders, the ones who truly change the game, aren't the ones with all the answers. They're the ones who ask the best questions. They know that *certainty* is a comfort zone and that *growth* happens in the unknown. They lean into ambiguity. They see failure as an experiment that provides new data.

And yet, too often, organizations and individuals build walls around creativity. They don't mean to (at least, not explicitly). But every time an idea is shut down before it's explored, every time someone is made to feel foolish for suggesting something new, and every time risk is treated as recklessness, another opportunity dies before it ever had the chance to take flight.

DOI: 10.4324/9781003627265-8

So, how do we build environments where ideas can soar? How do we foster cultures that make room for curiosity and experimentation? How do we move from playing it safe to playing to win?

In this chapter, we're going to break it down. We'll talk about what it takes to cultivate a space where ideas aren't just encouraged but actively nurtured. And explore the conditions that allow innovation to thrive: psychological safety, diverse thinking, and the ability to detach from ego and embrace exploration. We'll also shift the way we think about risk, about creativity, and about what it means to lead boldly.

Because creativity isn't magic, and you don't need a rabbit or a top hat. It's not reserved for the chosen few. You see, it's something that grows when given the right conditions, something that multiplies when shared. And when ideas are set free, when they're allowed to evolve, collide, stretch beyond their original form, that's when transformation happens.

Let's spark ideas and watch them fly.

Creativity and Innovation: The Foundation of Growth

Innovation begins with creativity or the ability to think differently, make connections between seemingly unrelated ideas, and imagine solutions beyond current limitations.[2]

But let's be honest for a moment, and you'll know this if you've ever tried to create something new. Fostering creativity in a structured work environment can be challenging. There are meetings to attend, deadlines to hit, and let's not forget the infamous *we've always done it this way* brigade.

Creativity doesn't thrive under red tape and rigid processes. It needs breathing room, a little playfulness, and the occasional 'bad' idea that turns out to be brilliant.

So, how do you spark innovation when your calendar looks like a game of Tetris? You start by making space, mentally and literally, for curiosity, experimentation, and the kind of thinking that dares to color outside the lines.

Balancing Divergent and Convergent Thinking

I once worked with a leader who had a mind like wildfire. Always moving, always expanding, always hungry for the next idea. He could see opportunity in the smallest of sparks, turning passing thoughts into something grander, something unexpected. His team loved his energy and his relentless belief that there was always a better way. But there was a problem. Without structure, without a process to filter and refine, most of those ideas never made it beyond the walls of the brainstorming room. They flickered out as quickly as they had appeared.

Innovation requires two distinct forces: **divergence** and **convergence**. Divergent thinking is the act of expansion, of generating possibilities without restraint. It's the meeting where every idea is valid, where no one says no, and where creativity is free to roam. It's essential. But on its own, it can leave ideas scattered, half-formed, and lacking traction.

That's where convergent thinking[3] comes in: the refinement process of narrowing possibilities into something tangible and executable. Without convergence, creativity remains an abstract exercise. Without divergence, it withers before it even begins.

Research[4] has shown that teams who alternate between these modes (expanding and contracting, exploring and executing) produce stronger, more effective results. They allow for the thrill of possibility without losing the discipline of action and create a cycle of innovation, where ideas can be turned into results.

Leaders who understand this balance create environments where creativity flourishes. They know when to let ideas run wild and when to shape them into something real. They design spaces where teams feel free to experiment while also ensuring that the best ideas don't get lost in the shuffle.

I've seen what happens when teams are given the time to think freely and to stretch their creative muscles without fear of judgment. The energy shifts. Conversations deepen. And most importantly, the ideas that come out of it don't just stay as ideas. They move. They take shape. They grow into something that wasn't there before.

That's the difference between wishful thinking and genuine innovation. After all, it's not just about dreaming big but also building the systems, mindset, and discipline to bring those dreams to life. And when leaders master this balance, when they create space for both exploration and execution, that's when they stop managing teams and start leading movements.

Creating an Environment for Creative Thinking

Early in my career, I worked for a company that seemed to operate on autopilot. The processes were efficient, and the results were predictable, but something was missing. Curiosity. The kind of curiosity that challenges assumptions and makes people lean in with interest, instead of checking out with indifference.

Years later, I led a team in an organization where innovation was the backbone of everything we did. We didn't just accept new ideas but actively created space for them and encouraged people to chase what fascinated them. Some of the most groundbreaking initiatives I've been part of weren't born in strategic planning sessions. They emerged in unexpected places: hallway conversations, impromptu brainstorms, and moments when people felt free to explore.

One well-known example of fostering creativity was Google's "20% Time Policy" and, more recently, Apple's "Blue Sky Program," which allowed employees to dedicate a portion of their workweek to passion projects. While few organizations may implement this exact model, the principle behind it is universal.

Big ideas emerge when people have the freedom to explore beyond immediate demands. Creativity needs space to breathe, not just a checklist of deliverables. A culture that values curiosity sparks innovation naturally, without forcing it into a rigid process.

The most forward-thinking leaders don't wait for inspiration to strike. They create conditions where new ideas can surface organically. Hackathons open the door to untapped creativity, encouraging possibilities that might not fit within a standard brainstorming session. Recognition isn't just about the final product. It celebrates bold thinking and the willingness to push boundaries. Environments designed for experimentation give people permission to contribute without fear of failure.

When innovation becomes part of everyday work, something shifts. People stop holding back. They lean in with their most original ideas, shaping solutions that redefine what's possible. That's when transformation happens.

Psychological Safety: The Foundation of Innovation

You can have the brightest minds in the room, the most ambitious goals, and the most compelling ideas. But if people don't feel safe to speak up, none of it will matter. Creativity thrives in an environment where people feel they won't be penalized for trying, failing, or thinking differently. Without psychological safety, innovation suffocates under the weight of fear.

Dr. Amy Edmondson[5] is a pioneer in research who has shown that psychological safety is one of the strongest predictors to maximize team and organizational performance. It allows individuals to take risks, propose ideas, and learn from setbacks without fear of blame. When people know they can contribute freely, they don't hold back. They challenge assumptions, voice their insights, and build upon each other's ideas. And that is where the magic happens.

One of the most powerful examples of psychological safety in action I've experienced was within a product development team I once worked with. They were tackling a complex problem, one that had been grappled with for years. But instead of walking on eggshells, fearful of suggesting something that might not work, this team thrived on open experimentation.

The leaders actively encouraged unfiltered brainstorming, making it clear that every idea had value. Some ideas led nowhere, others sparked new directions and became game-changers. That breakthrough wouldn't have happened in a fear-driven environment. It happened because people felt safe enough to take risks.

Leaders can foster psychological safety by encouraging openness, actively seeking input from all team members, and ensuring every voice is valued. They can share their experiences of trial and error, demonstrating that mistakes are part of the process. When leaders reward bold experimentation instead of just successful outcomes, they are letting the team know progress matters more than perfection. When failures occur, they can shift from blame to learning and turn setbacks into case studies to fuel future innovation.

Leveraging Cognitive Diversity for Innovation

The most transformative ideas don't come from environments where everyone thinks alike.[6] Breakthroughs happen when diverse perspectives, backgrounds, and ways of thinking intersect in spaces that welcome fresh input. Innovation thrives when a mix of problem-solving approaches, thought processes, and lived experiences come together.

Leveraging cognitive diversity, the range of how people analyze information, tackle challenges, and develop ideas, drives creativity in ways that often go unnoticed.[7] In fact, teams with high cognitive diversity are better equipped to tackle complex challenges, adapt to change, and develop creative solutions.[8]

I saw this play out firsthand during a global program rollout meant to standardize processes across multiple regions. What seemed like a well-designed, seamless plan at headquarters quickly ran into resistance on the ground. Some country leaders felt the global approach didn't account for their unique cultural and regulatory needs. Others worried that a one-size-fits-all model would strip away the nuances that made their local operations successful. What started as an ambitious initiative suddenly felt like a battle of perspectives.

Instead of forcing alignment, we changed the approach. We brought together a cross-functional team that included leaders from different countries, people who had been in the trenches, and those who had seen similar transformations succeed elsewhere. We created a space where concerns could be voiced openly, where differing viewpoints weren't just tolerated but valued.

At first, the conversations were difficult. People spoke candidly about what they believed wouldn't work. But as trust built, the discussion shifted. Instead of seeing the global rollout as imposed, the team saw an opportunity to co-create. We blended regional flexibility into the structure, allowing for adaptation while maintaining the overall framework. By the end, what had once seemed like an unworkable initiative became a model of collaboration. And the rollout's success wasn't because we insisted on a single point of view; it was because we made space for all of them.

Innovation thrives in environments where multiple perspectives are valued. Leaders who cultivate cognitive diversity assemble cross-functional teams, encourage debate without fear, and invite external voices to challenge assumptions. When people with different backgrounds, disciplines, and problem-solving approaches come together, they see possibilities that others miss.

Encouraging cognitive diversity takes more than good intentions. Thoughtful decisions shape teams that bring together different industries, disciplines, and viewpoints. The best ideas don't come from staying in familiar circles but actively seeking perspectives that challenge assumptions. Strong teams invite debate, welcome fresh thinking, and create an atmosphere where disagreement sparks progress rather than tension.

Some of the most impactful teams I've worked with were filled with strong opinions and contrasting viewpoints. Conversations didn't always flow smoothly. Ideas clashed. But that push and pull created breakthroughs that wouldn't have happened in a room full of like-minded thinkers. Innovation doesn't come from perfect harmony. The strongest ideas emerge when people step beyond their perspectives, wrestle with new ways of thinking, and commit to solving problems in unexpected ways. Leaders who embrace that process build cultures where breakthroughs become a natural outcome of how work gets done.

Embedding Innovation into Organizational Culture

Innovation doesn't come from a single brainstorming session or a corporate slogan. Fresh thinking takes root when problem-solving becomes second nature, shaping the way decisions are made and work gets done. Progress happens in places where people feel empowered to challenge assumptions, experiment with new ideas, and improve systems without waiting for approval.

Some organizations treat innovation as a buzzword, something leadership mentions in strategy meetings but rarely puts into practice. A different energy exists in teams where creativity is expected, not just encouraged. Walking into those spaces, the shift is obvious. Conversations feel alive with possibility. People push boundaries, question long-standing processes, and search for better solutions as part of their daily work. The mindset isn't about asking for permission but making things better.

Cultures that foster innovation don't rely on occasional bursts of creativity. Leadership plays a role in setting the tone by welcoming fresh perspectives, recognizing effort, and seeing setbacks as learning moments rather than failures. When people feel safe to experiment, ideas flow freely, and continuous improvement becomes a natural part of the environment.

Creating Safe-to-Fail Environments

Innovation thrives in places where people feel free to explore the unknown without fear of punishment. The most forward-thinking leaders create *safe-to-fail* projects: spaces where bold experimentation is not only allowed but also celebrated. It's about carving out controlled environments where ideas can be tested, where failure isn't seen as failure but as insight gained.

Years ago, I worked with a team testing a completely new operational model. One that, if successful, could drastically improve efficiency and reduce cost. But the risks were high, and the stakes even higher. Instead of demanding immediate success, leadership framed the initiative as an experiment. The team was given room to pivot, tweak, and test without the looming threat of failure killing momentum. And because they had that space, they refined their approach until they found a model that worked and became a new standard.

Building Continuous Feedback Loops

Innovation moves forward only when organizations refuse to stand still. Sometimes, fresh ideas emerge through bold experimentation. Other times, progress comes from refining what already exists. Systems designed for continuous improvement don't rely on chance. Every effort builds toward something greater when strong feedback loops turn past experiences into valuable insights that shape future decisions.

Meanwhile, methodologies like the lean startup model emphasize rapid prototyping and real-time learning. Yet, these principles extend far beyond product development. Across leadership and strategy, teams that pause to assess what works, where obstacles appear, and what adjustments will lead to better outcomes stay ahead of the curve.

Likewise, curiosity transforms post-project reviews from routine check-ins to powerful learning moments. Instead of simply closing the book on completed work, great leaders ask the right questions. *What drove success? Where did the momentum stall?* How can lessons from today strengthen the next challenge? Success deserves more than celebration. Breaking it apart, studying the patterns, and refining the approach make every achievement a foundation for the next breakthrough.

Incentivizing Creativity

Motivation looks different for everyone. Some people respond to financial rewards, while others find inspiration in autonomy, recognition, or a strong sense of purpose. Research suggests that understanding what drives individuals matters more than applying a one-size-fits-all approach to incentives. A study published in 2024[9] found that when people have the choice between cash and non-cash rewards in crowdsourcing contests, creative performance improves significantly. The takeaway? Customization fuels innovation.

Teams that consistently produce groundbreaking ideas thrive in environments where effort is valued, not just outcomes. Acknowledging the courage to experiment, the persistence to refine ideas, and the curiosity to challenge assumptions fosters a culture where people feel encouraged to think differently. Ownership over projects deepens commitment. The freedom to explore possibilities strengthens confidence.

Fostering Cross-Disciplinary Collaboration

Breakthrough ideas rarely emerge in isolation. The most exciting innovations take shape when different disciplines, backgrounds, and ways of thinking intersect. Bringing together diverse expertise unlocks new perspectives that wouldn't have surfaced in a room full of like-minded people.

A project team I worked with faced a challenge that had been lingering for months. Safety leaders and engineers had exhausted every traditional approach, yet the problem remained unsolved. Conversations felt circular, solutions felt limited, and frustration was starting to set in. Instead of repeating the same discussions, a decision was made to bring in fresh voices from marketing, behavioral science, and even UX design.

Skepticism filled the room at first. Some believed the technical nature of the issue required only subject matter experts, while others questioned what an outsider could offer. Once the dialogue began, everything changed. A marketing strategist reframed the problem as a communication challenge rather than an engineering flaw. A UX designer introduced concepts from human-centered design that had never been considered. Within days, ideas surfaced that no single team would have reached alone.

Encouraging collaboration across disciplines doesn't require a massive restructuring. Simple shifts, such as inviting different teams into problem-solving sessions, rotating perspectives in leadership meetings, or pairing unlikely partners on projects, create environments where curiosity thrives. Organizations that embrace this approach don't treat innovation as a one-time initiative or a flashy campaign. Making space for unexpected connections, challenging assumptions, and welcoming new ways of thinking turns innovation into an everyday practice.

Sustaining Innovation for Lasting Impact

Ideas need more than a single spark to create lasting change. A brainstorming session, a breakthrough moment, or a bold experiment might start the process, but momentum keeps progress alive. The strongest organizations move beyond innovation as an isolated event and embed fresh thinking into daily work, shaping the way teams solve problems, challenge assumptions, and push boundaries.

Throughout this chapter, curiosity, experimentation, and diverse thinking have emerged as the foundations of creativity. Psychological safety creates the trust needed for bold ideas to surface. A growth mindset shifts setbacks into opportunities for learning. But generating ideas is only the beginning. Without resilience, even the most promising innovations struggle to gain traction. Setbacks happen. Some ideas require refining. Others may not work at all. The teams that create the biggest impact approach challenges as stepping stones rather than barriers, adjusting, testing again, and moving forward with new insights.

One of the most innovative teams I worked with was not the most well-funded, the most experienced, or the most technically advanced. Strength came from an ability to treat every challenge as an opportunity to improve. When an experiment failed, the conversation immediately turned to lessons learned, adjustments needed, and what came next. That mindset made the difference between an idea that fades and one that evolves into something bigger.

The next chapter explores resilience and how to use it as a tool for transformation. The strongest leaders step into the unknown, knowing that every failure, every pivot, and every unexpected turn holds the potential for something even greater.

Notes

1 I am a named inventor on U.S. Patent No. 11,769,110, *Systems and Methods for Operator Motion Management*, granted on September 26, 2023. The patent, assigned to Amazon Technologies, Inc., describes methods for utilizing video input data and machine learning models to generate kinematic data and improve operator motion management.

2 Sawyer, R. K. 2012. *Explaining Creativity: The Science of Human Innovation* (2nd ed.). Oxford University Press.

3 Cropley, A. 2006. "In Praise of Convergent Thinking." *Creativity Research Journal* 18(3): 391–404.

4 Basadur, M., and G. Gelade. 2006. "The Role of Knowledge Management in the Innovation Process." *Creativity and Innovation Management* 15(1): 45–62.

5 Edmondson, A. C. 2018. *The Fearless Organization: Creating Psychological Safety in the Workplace for Learning, Innovation, and Growth*. Wiley.

6 Hewlett, S. A., M. Marshall, and L. Sherbin. 2013. "How Diversity Can Drive Innovation." *Harvard Business Review* 91(12): 30–41.
7 Page, S. E. 2007. *The Difference: How the Power of Diversity Creates Better Groups, Firms, Schools, and Societies.* Princeton University Press.
8 Rock, D., H. Grant, and J. Grey. 2016. "Diverse Teams Feel Less Comfortable - And That's Why They Perform Better." *Harvard Business Review* 94(9): 62–67.
9 Riedl, C., J. Füller, K. Hutter, and G. J. Tellis. 2024. "Cash or Non-Cash? Exploring Ideators' Incentive Preferences in Crowdsourcing Contests." *Journal of Management Information Systems* 41(2): 487–514. https://doi.org/10.1080/07421222.2024.2340828.

Chapter 8

Strengths You Can't See but Feel

I remember the moment with absolute clarity. The realization that this wasn't going to be my forever company. The job I had worked so hard to get, the one that seemed like the pinnacle of everything I had built, wasn't the finish line I once imagined. I wouldn't be retiring from here.

That thought came suddenly, like the sharp intake of breath before stepping into icy water. The realization wasn't dramatic, but it was profound. A quiet, slow unraveling of certainty, the way the tide gently pulls back from the shore before you even notice it's receding. I was sitting in my office, staring at the walls covered in ideas and scribbles, a quiet space amid the hum of a high-performance culture. I had built something here: a team, a strategy, a rhythm. I had fought for ideas, pushed boundaries, and led with conviction. And yet, deep down, I knew. This wasn't the end of my story, just another chapter.

A close colleague caught me staring out the window long after most had left for the day. The office lights reflected off the glass. They leaned against the doorframe, their voice soft but knowing. "You okay?"

I exhaled, turning toward them. "I thought this was it. The dream job. The one where I'd stay, grow, finish my career. But now, I'm not so sure."

They studied me for a moment, then stepped inside, lowering their voice as if sharing a secret. "I know that feeling. It's unsettling. But maybe that's the point. Maybe it's not about staying in one place. It's about what you do while you're here."

Their words settled over me and filled the space left by my uncertainty. *What now?* That was the real question. It wasn't about what was next on the career ladder or where I'd land. It was about something deeper, about how I would show up despite knowing this chapter had an expiration date.

Resilience, I realized, wasn't just about pushing through hardship. It wasn't about gritting my teeth and enduring. It was about standing firm when the ground beneath me shifted, about finding a way to keep leading, inspiring, and building, even when the future was uncertain. Resilience was about grace under pressure. It was about leading not just for personal

DOI: 10.4324/9781003627265-9

success but for impact. For the people who relied on me, for the work that still mattered, and for the legacy I could leave behind long after I was gone.

So I did what I knew best: I leaned in. I led my team with the same passion, the same fire. I built them up, knowing that the impact we made together would outlast my time there. I delivered results. Not for job security, not to prove anything, but because that's who I was. That's what resilience demanded of me.

In that process, I became a better leader. A more compassionate one. When you lead through uncertainty, you see people differently. You recognize their own struggles, their own fears about change. You learn to steady them when they waver and remind them of their own strength when they doubt it. Resilience isn't just about surviving the storm but guiding others through it, ensuring they come out stronger, braver, and more capable on the other side.

In this chapter, we'll go beyond platitudes and explore the topic of resilience. How it's built, sustained, and how leaders can cultivate it within themselves and their teams. We'll talk about how to navigate setbacks, how to keep moving when the road ahead is unclear, and how to turn challenges into catalysts for growth. Because leadership isn't just about vision. It's about endurance. And the strongest leaders? They don't just survive change. They rise within it.

Resilience: A Leadership Imperative

Resilience operates at every level: individual, organizational, and societal. Leaders, businesses, and entire nations must continuously strengthen their capacity to withstand shocks, adapt to uncertainty, and emerge stronger from disruption. Without intentional investment, resilience remains fragile, leaving people, institutions, and economies vulnerable to external pressures.

At a **macro level**, global challenges such as geopolitical shifts, climate change, and economic instability demand structural resilience. Governments and industries must build adaptive policies, diversified economies, and agile systems that endure prolonged uncertainty.

Indeed, the *WEF Resilience Pulse Check 2025*[1] highlights a concerning gap that while 84% of companies feel unprepared for future disruptions, only 13% have embedded resilience into strategic decision-making. Many governments and businesses still prioritize immediate recovery rather than long-term preparedness, leaving economic and institutional frameworks exposed to instability.

At a **micro level**, businesses and individuals face their own versions of volatility. Organizations must develop internal structures for flexibility, knowledge-sharing, and risk mitigation. Employees need environments that support psychological safety, continuous learning, and adaptive thinking, which we discussed in Chapter 7.

The *Resilience Pulse Check* reveals that companies focus heavily on financial and digital resilience but often neglect human resilience, failing to invest in leadership development, workforce adaptability, and cultural readiness for change. A business that prioritizes systems over people weakens its ability to sustain innovation and long-term performance.

Leaders carry the responsibility of bridging these levels of resilience. Adapting to shifting markets and technological advances requires more than operational agility. It demands **personal resilience,** the ability to manage stress, make decisions under pressure, and sustain energy through uncertainty. Resilient leadership fosters team confidence, ensuring that businesses do not merely react to change but anticipate and shape it.

Yet, **organizational resilience** cannot exist without investment in individuals. A culture that encourages experimentation, rewards learning from failure, and nurtures adaptive thinking creates a workforce capable of navigating uncertainty. Strong businesses contribute to resilient economies. Countries with robust infrastructure, crisis-ready institutions, and forward-thinking policies create stability for businesses and individuals alike.

Resilience, whether at a national, business, or personal level, is not a fixed trait. Adaptability grows through repeated exposure to challenge, the willingness to reframe setbacks as learning moments, and the ability to act rather than react. The future belongs to those who see change not as a disruption to endure but as an opportunity to redefine what comes next.

Strategies for Cultivating Resilience

One way to think about resilience is as a muscle that strengthens through intentional practice, conscious adaptation, and the willingness to meet adversity head-on. Leaders who cultivate resilience within themselves and their teams shape an environment where challenges transform into stepping stones for growth. True resilience is built on a foundation of mindset, adaptability, and collective strength.

Developing a Growth Mindset

We discussed having a growth mindset in Chapter 2. A leader's mindset shapes the culture of their team. Those who view challenges as opportunities rather than roadblocks cultivate an organization that thrives on perseverance. A growth mindset, the belief that abilities and intelligence can be developed, fuels a resilient team where setbacks are no longer failures but lessons embedded in the learning process.

In a high-stakes project I once led, we faced a seemingly insurmountable hurdle: a client rejecting a solution into which we had poured months of effort. Instead of frustration, we reframed it as an opportunity. *What had we missed? Where could we improve?* The team dissected the setback, uncovered blind spots, and restructured the solution. When we presented it again, not only did the client accept it, but they also expanded the contract. That moment solidified a truth: resilience isn't just about acceptance. It's about continuous improvement and an unwavering belief that growth comes from challenge.

To instill this within a team, leaders must normalize risk-taking. They create environments where employees can experiment without fear, ensuring that even setbacks are met with curiosity rather than criticism. Celebrating progress rather than just results reinforces the notion that resilience is not about never failing. It's about never ceasing to learn.

Building Mental Agility through Reframing

Resilient leaders understand that perception shapes response. The ability to cognitively reframe a challenge. In other words, seeing it through multiple lenses determines whether a team will see adversity as a threat or an opportunity.

During a global crisis, I worked with a leader whose team faced sudden layoffs and an overwhelming sense of uncertainty. Instead of allowing the uncertainty to create paralysis, she shifted the narrative. *What can we control? What resources do we still have?* By guiding her team to focus on what was within their power, she turned panic into problem-solving. They identified new efficiencies, pivoted their strategy, and ultimately positioned themselves to emerge stronger when conditions stabilized.

This ability to reframe obstacles fuels mental agility, the capacity to shift perspectives, remain open to new solutions, and reimagine pathways to success. Leaders model this by asking questions that expand thinking, *How else can we see this situation? What's the upside we haven't considered?* By embedding cognitive flexibility into everyday problem-solving, they build a team culture that doesn't just endure setbacks but adapts dynamically to change.

Fostering a Collaborative and Supportive Environment

Resilience is not an individual pursuit. It actually thrives in the community. The strongest teams are those built on trust, shared purpose, and the knowledge that they don't face challenges alone. Leaders must create environments where team members feel safe to voice concerns, share struggles, and lean on each other during times of uncertainty.

We discussed the concept of *psychological safety* in Chapter 7, which applies equally here.

One organization I worked with implemented a practice called *resilience huddles,* weekly sessions where employees discussed not only their work challenges but also their personal stressors. These meetings became a space of mutual support, reinforcing that resilience is not about going it alone but about drawing strength from those around you. The impact was undeniable: morale improved, collaboration deepened, and the team developed a collective endurance that allowed them to navigate major disruptions with unity rather than fear.

Encouraging peer mentorship, open dialogue, and shared wins fosters an environment where resilience is not just an individual trait but a collective strength. Leaders must reinforce that resilience is not about solitary endurance but about lifting each other in the moments that test us the most.

Leveraging Agile Methodologies to Enhance Adaptability

Agility and resilience go hand in hand. The ability to pivot, iterate, and respond fluidly to new information determines whether an organization can withstand disruption or be destroyed by it. Agile methodologies, which are rooted in iteration, collaboration, and responsiveness, offer a framework for embedding resilience into organizational culture.

One leader I coached spearheaded a major transformation within her company's operations. She didn't roll out a rigid, one-size-fits-all strategy. Instead, she introduced an agile approach. She broke the initiative into phases, gathering feedback in real time, and adjusted it based on team insights. The result? A more adaptive, engaged workforce that saw change not as a disruption but as a continuous evolution.

Resilient organizations do not wait for stability before making decisions. They build structures that allow for movement, creating systems that prioritize flexibility over rigidity. Leaders reinforce this by encouraging iterative learning and cross-functional collaboration, where diverse insights fuel creative problem-solving. Adaptability is not a reaction to change; it's a proactive strategy for adjusting an ever-evolving landscape.

Building Resilience Reserves to Manage Future Disruptions

Much like an athlete conditions their body for endurance, organizations must build resilience reserves or strategic buffers to withstand unexpected turbulence. These reserves take many forms: cross-trained employees who can step into multiple roles, financial safeguards that provide stability in downturns, and external partnerships that serve as additional support systems.

In one company facing a sudden downturn, leadership had the foresight to have resilience reserves in place: employees were cross-trained in multiple functions, financial reserves allowed for strategic pivots without immediate cuts, and partnerships enabled shared resources. While competitors faltered, this organization adapted seamlessly, using its reserves to weather the storm while planning for long-term growth.

Leaders must think beyond the immediate and anticipate future disruptions, ensuring their organizations have the structural resilience to not just survive challenges but seize opportunities within them. This forward-thinking approach ensures that resilience is not just a reaction to adversity but a defining strength in an organization's operations.

The Resilient Leader's Mindset

Resilient leaders are more than just survivors of disruption. They are architects of transformation. They understand that how they respond to challenges sets the tone for those around them. Their teams look to them not for perfection, but for steadiness, clarity, and conviction. And so, they cultivate a mindset that doesn't merely endure adversity but actively reshapes it into opportunity.

You will remember that we discussed boldness in Chapter 4. Boldness and resilience are deeply connected, though they manifest in different ways. Resilience is the ability to withstand, adapt, and grow through adversity, while boldness is the courage to take risks, challenge norms, and step into the unknown.

However, one cannot exist without the other. This is because boldness fuels resilience. When faced with uncertainty or setbacks, it takes boldness to keep moving forward instead of retreating into fear. At the same time, boldness becomes fuel for reinvention, and resilient leaders boldly reshape their circumstances, refusing to accept limitations.

Bold leaders get knocked down. A lot. But without resilience, boldness crumbles at the first setback. Bold leaders invite risk, failure, and criticism. Resilience ensures a leader can handle setbacks without losing confidence.

The best leaders embody both boldness and resilience. Leaders who are only bold but not resilient burn out quickly or give up when things don't go their way. Leaders who are resilient but not bold may survive, but they won't create a lasting impact because they will avoid the courageous moves that drive transformation. The most transformative leaders are bold enough to take risks and resilient enough to handle setbacks.

And resilient leaders know that setbacks are not endpoints but pivots. When uncertainty arises, they don't dwell on what has been lost. Instead, they ask, *What is still within our control? What can we build from here?* Their energy is directed toward solutions, turning obstacles into catalysts for reinvention.

Adaptability over Rigidity

Resilience provides the foundation, but adaptability builds the framework for sustained success. In a world that constantly shifts, leaders who cling to past strategies risk falling behind. The most effective decision-makers remain flexible, adjusting their course while staying true to a larger vision. Outdated approaches hold no place in environments where progress demands continuous learning, bold pivots, and a willingness to embrace the unknown with curiosity rather than hesitation.

A strong leader understands that stability does not mean standing still. Trust, clarity, and purpose create steady ground, not resistance to change. Cultures that encourage agility empower people to experiment, refine ideas, and evolve with the landscape. Workplaces that foster adaptability develop teams prepared not only to withstand disruption but also to drive innovation through uncertainty.

Empathy and Support: The Human Side of Resilience

Strategies alone do not build resilience. People do. The strongest leaders recognize that resilience is a shared effort, cultivated not just through systems but through human connection. Understanding that challenges create uncertainty, great leaders offer more than direction by providing reassurance, belonging, and trust.

A mentor once demonstrated this through a deceptively simple habit. Before launching any change, a single question set the tone: *How are you feeling about this?* That moment was never rushed or superficial. Space was created for fears, concerns, and emotions to surface without hesitation. Vulnerability became a strength, reinforcing trust, strengthening cohesion, and making resilience a shared experience.

Leadership in adversity requires more than perseverance. Pausing to acknowledge the weight of change fosters commitment. Recognizing the emotional toll of uncertainty ensures that no one carries the burden alone. Cultures built on support, trust, and open dialogue sustain resilience far beyond a single challenge, creating a strong foundation no matter what comes next.

Resilience as a Catalyst for Sustainable Success

Resilience is more than standing firm when the ground shifts. Moving with purpose, adjusting with clarity, and carrying forward the lessons that hardship has to offer to define the leaders who make a lasting impact. Strength does not come from avoiding adversity but from learning how to shape challenges into catalysts for growth. Every experience, no matter how difficult, provides an opportunity to sharpen vision and deepen influence.

Teams empowered to think boldly, challenge assumptions, and embrace reinvention move beyond survival into sustained success. The difference between those who endure and those who lead comes down to mindset, the ability to meet disruption with steady hands, clear direction, and a willingness to evolve.

But resilience alone does not create lasting change. Strength without purpose becomes endurance, and endurance without meaning leads nowhere. The most impactful leaders move beyond persistence, ensuring that every trial contributes to something greater. Aligning resilience with a broader mission shapes not only personal growth but also the future of those who follow.

And so, we turn our conversation back to purpose, the thread woven through every decision, every risk, and every act of courage. The next chapter explores leadership that moves beyond challenges and into transformation. Resilience shaped by purpose does not just withstand change. That kind of leadership defines the future.

Note

1 World Economic Forum. 2025. *Resilience Pulse Check 2025: Assessing Organizational Preparedness for an Uncertain Future.* World Economic Forum.

Chapter 9

Heart First, Always

Exhaustion settled over me, heavier than fatigue, the kind that no amount of rest could erase. Sitting alone in my car, hands resting on the steering wheel as I waited for my son to finish his gymnastics practice, a quiet but persistent question surfaced. *Why am I doing this*? The weight pressing down wasn't from long hours or difficult decisions, although that was a daily challenge.

Something deeper had shifted.

Purpose had faded into routine, misalignment creeping in so gradually that I hadn't noticed until then. Leadership had once felt clear and intentional, but somewhere along the way, that clarity had unraveled, leaving behind only the motions of responsibility without the conviction that once fueled them.

Leading at the highest levels meant managing global teams, driving massive initiatives, and delivering results that looked like success from the outside. Every metric, every milestone, every external measure said I was excelling. But beneath the surface, something had shifted. My focus had narrowed to outcomes. Targets hit, projects completed, and expectations met. Progress had become the measure of my worth, and in that pursuit, something essential had faded: the *why* behind it all.

That quiet moment in my car forced a reckoning. A harder question surfaced – *was I leading in a way that truly reflected my values?* Stripping away titles, deliverables, and the constant chase for achievement, the honest answer was no. The drive to create impact, to elevate others, and to spark meaningful change had been drowned out by external demands. The voice that once guided me with conviction had been replaced by the relentless push for results. A choice stood before me: continue leading from a place of expectation or realign, recalibrate, and return to leadership that meant something deeper.

True leadership isn't about metrics. The foundation is built on alignment, where actions reflect values and where leadership moves beyond performance to purpose. That kind of leadership doesn't start with numbers.

DOI: 10.4324/9781003627265-10

It starts with heart. Always.

A world that celebrates short-term wins and immediate returns often pulls leaders away from what really matters. Momentum builds around results, numbers, and fleeting achievements, yet the most transformative leaders, the ones who redefine industries, ignite change, and leave legacies, are anchored to something else.

This chapter extends an invitation to lead with greater intention. A call to look inward, to reflect on what fuels ambition, and to define the impact that leadership will leave behind. Conversations will explore how purpose shapes culture, strengthens resilience, and elevates teams. Authentic leadership, rooted in courage, conviction, and heart, creates ripples that extend far beyond any single decision, forging a legacy that outlives the moment and leaves an imprint that lasts.

Why Purpose Matters

Leadership without purpose is like sailing without a map. You may move forward, but the destination is uncertain, and the journey is dictated by external forces rather than intentional direction. Purpose-driven leadership is understanding *why* those goals matter, why the work itself is meaningful, and why staying the course through challenges is worth it.

A leader's purpose is an internal compass, guiding every choice, shaping every priority, and influencing every action. When purpose runs deep, it fuels not just individual resolve but collective energy. Teams feel the presence of a leader who operates with conviction. That clarity resonates in the way decisions unfold, the way obstacles are approached, and the way people are inspired to move forward together.

Moments of turbulence test even the most resilient leaders. Without a clear sense of purpose, it's easy to become reactive, chasing immediate solutions while losing sight of the long-term vision. Leaders who remain rooted in purpose approach uncertainty with steadiness. Focus shifts from the immediate challenge to the broader mission, ensuring that setbacks do not dictate the path forward. Purpose sustains momentum, providing the clarity needed to push through uncertainty and lead with intention rather than impulse.

According to Gallup's study on purpose,[1] employees who see a connection between their values and the organization's mission report higher satisfaction and are more likely to go above and beyond in their roles. It makes sense. When people feel that what they do matters, they invest more of themselves into it.

They don't just work for a paycheck, they work for impact. But speaking of a paycheck and financial performance, it's probably no surprise that companies that prioritize purpose outperform those that operate without a clear sense of direction. Research[2] consistently shows that organizations with a well-defined purpose experience stronger financial returns, increased employee engagement, and greater long-term stability. When employees connect their daily work to a mission beyond profits, productivity rises, innovation accelerates, and turnover declines. Purpose acts as both a motivator and a differentiator, fueling commitment and driving performance at every level.

Purpose also strengthens resilience in times of economic uncertainty. Companies that embed purpose into decision-making frameworks respond more effectively to disruption, adapting strategies with long-term value in mind rather than reacting solely to short-term market pressures. Investors recognize this advantage, leading to a better brand reputation, increased stakeholder trust, and ultimately, a more sustainable financial trajectory.

The connection between purpose and performance is measurable, repeatable, and undeniable. When organizations align financial goals with a clear mission, they don't just survive market fluctuations; they thrive, setting new benchmarks for success while creating meaningful impact.

The Core Components of Purpose-Driven Leadership

At the heart of purpose-driven leadership are three essential elements: a clear personal mission, alignment with the broader values of an organization, and the ability to communicate that purpose in a way that resonates. Together, these components create a foundation for leadership that not only ignites inspiration but also fosters lasting impact.

Clarifying Your Leadership Mission

A leader's purpose is not found in job descriptions or performance metrics. It is discovered through deep introspection and becomes the force that keeps you grounded when external pressures rise. Defining a clear purpose requires honesty, vulnerability, and a willingness to ask difficult questions.

According to Quinn and Thakor[3] in the *Harvard Business Review*, leaders who cultivate a clear organizational purpose exhibit greater authenticity, self-awareness, and consistency in their decision-making, fostering a more engaged and committed workforce.

So, how can you apply this in practice? Consider these questions when you're clarifying your purpose:

What are my core values?

What beliefs define me and serve as my guide in both leadership and life?

What motivates me to lead?

What change do I want to see, and how do I contribute to it?

How do I want to be remembered?
What lasting impact do I want to leave behind?

Aligning Purpose with Organizational Vision and Goals

Purpose-driven leadership doesn't operate in isolation. The most effective leaders bridge the gap between personal purpose and organizational mission, ensuring their leadership uplifts and unifies those around them. When leaders connect their purpose to their organization's broader vision, they create an alignment that mobilizes teams toward a shared goal.

Deloitte[4] reveals that organizations with strong purpose alignment experience greater resilience and adaptability, as employees are unified by a collective mission that transcends individual roles.

To create this alignment, leaders must communicate purpose consistently and integrate it into daily operations. Simon Sinek's "Golden Circle" framework[5] reinforces the importance of starting with *why* – ensuring that every action and decision is rooted in a larger purpose before addressing *how* and *what*.

Modeling Purpose in Action

The most compelling leaders do not just talk about purpose. They live it. They model authenticity, demonstrating through action what purpose-driven leadership looks like. Research shows that leaders who embody purpose inspire greater trust and loyalty, fostering a culture rooted in authenticity and commitment.[6]

A supply chain executive I worked with faced a defining moment when choosing between a supplier who offered lower costs and one that adhered to fair-trade standards. He chose the ethical supplier, despite the higher price, because it aligned with his company's values. But he didn't stop there. He openly communicated the decision to his employees, explaining how it reinforced their mission of responsible business practices. The result? His team became even more engaged and proud to work for a company that stood by its principles.

Purpose-driven leadership requires commitment, clarity, and the courage to align one's leadership with what truly matters. As we continue through this chapter, we will explore how purpose-driven leadership influences culture, strengthens resilience, and fosters long-term impact, ensuring that leadership is not just about achieving results, but about creating lasting change.

The Impact of Purpose on Organizational Culture

Purpose-driven leadership is not just a leadership philosophy. It is the foundation of a thriving, engaged, and future-focused organization. When purpose is embedded within an organization's culture, it creates a self-reinforcing cycle of meaning, motivation, and shared success.

Purpose as a Driver of Engagement and Retention

The most engaged employees feel deeply connected to the mission of their work. When people believe in the purpose behind what they do, they contribute with passion, creativity, and a sense of ownership.

A report by McKinsey[7] highlights that employees in purpose-driven organizations are more engaged, productive, and loyal. When people feel that their work is connected to something greater than themselves, they show up differently. They bring more energy, more commitment, and ownership over their contributions. Purpose becomes a cultural force that aligns individual motivation with organizational vision, creating an environment where personal and collective goals intertwine.

A global retail company struggling with high employee attrition discovered this firsthand. After a deep internal review, leadership realized employees felt disconnected from the company's values. In response, they made a strategic shift, aligning leadership messaging, training programs, and recognition initiatives around the company's deeper purpose: creating sustainable and ethical shopping experiences. Within a year, employee engagement scores rose, and retention improved significantly. The lesson was clear: when employees see their work as part of a larger mission, they stay. Not out of obligation but because they believe in the impact they're making.

Purpose as a Catalyst for Innovation and Adaptability

Purpose also propels organizations forward. Companies with a clearly defined purpose are more agile and innovative because they operate with a long-term vision that transcends short-term fluctuations. When teams understand *why* they are innovating, they push boundaries, take smart risks, and focus on solutions that create real impact.

Purpose-driven organizations foster collaboration and innovation by encouraging employees to think beyond day-to-day tasks and embrace a mindset of continuous improvement.[8] Purpose creates a culture where change is not feared but embraced as a necessary step toward fulfilling a greater mission.

Consider a technology company committed to bridging the digital divide in underserved communities. Because its purpose is clear, employees are empowered to challenge conventional product strategies, finding ways to create affordable, high-impact solutions. Innovation flourishes in this type of culture. Not just because leadership encourages it but because employees see their work as part of a greater transformation.

Purpose as a Pillar for Building Resilience

As discussed in Chapter 8, resilience is essential for navigating disruption. But resilience without purpose is unsustainable. Purpose gives teams a clear *why* that anchors them during uncertainty, preventing burnout and fostering a collective sense of mission.

In moments of crisis, purpose-driven organizations help their teams see beyond the immediate difficulty and stay focused on long-term impact. Employees who feel connected to a meaningful mission are more likely to persist through obstacles because they understand that setbacks are temporary but their contributions have lasting value.

During the early months of the COVID-19 pandemic, a logistics company faced massive disruptions. Rather than defaulting to survival mode, leadership reinforced the company's mission: ensuring critical supply chains remained intact to support essential businesses. This renewed sense of purpose became a rallying force. Employees at all levels worked collaboratively to implement creative solutions, maintaining service levels despite unprecedented challenges. Because they saw their work as vital, they remained engaged and resilient, ensuring the company survived and strengthened its industry standing.

Purpose-driven leadership transforms organizational culture at every level. It fuels engagement, sparks innovation, and reinforces resilience, creating an environment where employees are not just present but fully invested. When purpose is ingrained in daily operations, it becomes more than a statement, it becomes the force that sustains motivation, drives progress, and ensures that leadership is not just about direction, but about lasting impact.

Actionable Steps to Foster Purpose-Driven Leadership

Leading with purpose means turning vision into daily action. Decisions, culture, and team energy all reflect a commitment to meaningful impact. Purpose comes to life through consistent leadership, shaping every interaction and guiding every choice. The strategies ahead will help reinforce alignment, build momentum, and create a leadership approach that inspires and sustains lasting impact.

Clearly Articulate and Communicate Your Purpose

Effective leadership requires a constant reinforcement of purpose. Not just in words, but in actions. Leaders who consistently communicate the "why" behind their decisions create clarity and alignment, ensuring that purpose is not just a concept but a lived experience within their teams.

One of the simplest yet most powerful ways to reinforce purpose is through storytelling. When leaders share real-life examples illustrating how purpose-driven decisions have created a meaningful impact, whether for customers, employees, or the broader community, they make purpose tangible. Purpose-driven leaders also integrate their mission into daily operations, starting team meetings with a reflection on how their work contributes to a greater goal, ensuring the mission remains front and center.

Connect Purpose to Performance Goals

Purpose strengthens when woven into measurable goals, creating a direct link between daily efforts and a broader mission. When people understand how their contributions drive meaningful outcomes, motivation and engagement naturally rise. Leaders can reinforce this connection by integrating purpose into performance conversations, setting milestones that highlight the real impact, and consistently showing how everyday responsibilities contribute to the organization's larger vision. By making purpose a guiding thread rather than an abstract concept, leadership fosters a culture where work feels more meaningful and success is measured not just by outcomes but by the difference made along the way.

For instance, in a technology company committed to bridging the digital divide, leadership might tie performance metrics to accessibility improvements, measuring success not just by revenue, but by the number of underserved communities gaining access to technology. When employees see how their work drives real change, their sense of ownership deepens, fueling a culture of innovation and purpose-driven progress.

Recognize Purpose-Driven Achievements

Celebrating purpose-driven contributions reinforces the values that shape an organization's identity. Leaders who recognize and reward employees for embodying purpose create a culture where values-driven work is encouraged and expected.

Recognition can take many forms, from formal awards to informal acknowledgments. Some organizations establish "Purpose Awards," recognizing individuals who go beyond their roles to advance the company's mission. Others use public platforms, such as internal newsletters, team meetings, or social media, to highlight employees who demonstrate purpose-driven leadership in action. This acknowledgment validates efforts and inspires others to align their actions with the organization's core values.

Foster a Growth-Oriented Environment

Purpose-driven leadership flourishes in environments that embrace learning and adaptability. Creating opportunities for growth allows individuals to strengthen their skills, tackle meaningful challenges, and deepen the connection between their work and personal values.

Supporting professional development through training programs, mentorship, and purpose-aligned projects builds engagement and commitment. Meaningful conversations that encourage reflection help team members recognize how their contributions support a larger mission. When individuals see the impact of their work and feel empowered to apply their strengths in meaningful ways, a shared sense of purpose becomes a driving force within the organization.

Purpose as the Anchor of Enduring Leadership

Leadership shaped by purpose reaches beyond strategies and short-term wins. A deep connection links values with vision, weaving resilience, authenticity, and impact into the fabric of an organization. Purpose brings clarity in uncertainty, strengthens commitment through adversity, and transforms workplaces into environments where innovation, engagement, and meaningful progress flourish.

Throughout this chapter, the power of purpose has been explored as a driving force behind decisions, a source of inspiration for teams, and a foundation that sustains momentum. Leadership grounded in purpose does more than achieve results; it shapes cultures, fosters deep connections, and turns challenges into opportunities for lasting impact.

Looking ahead, purpose does not stand alone. Legacy emerges when purpose transforms into action that outlives a single leader, a single initiative, or a single moment in time. The next chapter moves beyond the present, focusing on the lasting influence leaders leave behind. The decisions made today ripple forward, shaping organizations, industries, and the people who will carry the vision into the future. Let leadership be more than a role, let it be a legacy.

Notes

1 Gallup. 2020. *The Relationship between Engagement at Work and Organizational Outcomes: 2020 Q12® Meta-Analysis* (10th ed.). Gallup, Inc.
2 Gartenberg, C., A. Prat, & G. Serafeim. 2019. "Corporate Purpose and Financial Performance." *Organization Science* 30(1): 1–18. https://doi.org/10.1287/orsc.2018.1230.
3 Quinn, R. E., and A. V. Thakor. 2018. "Creating a Purpose-Driven Organization." *Harvard Business Review* 96(4): 78–85.

4 Deloitte. 2021. *Building the Resilient Organization: 2021 Deloitte Global Resilience Report*. Deloitte Touche Tohmatsu Limited. https://www2.deloitte.com/us/en/insights/topics/strategy/characteristics-resilient-organizations.html.
5 Sinek, S. 2009. *Start with Why: How Great Leaders Inspire Everyone to Take Action*. Penguin.
6 Hollensbe, E., C. Wookey, L. Hickey, G. George, and V. Nichols. 2014. "Organizations with Purpose: From the Particular to the Universal." *Academy of Management Journal* 57(5): 1227–1234.
7 Dhingra, N., J. Emmett, A. Samo, and B. Schaninger. 2021. "Help Your Employees Find Purpose – Or Watch Them Leave." *McKinsey & Company*, April 5. https://www.mckinsey.com/capabilities/people-and-organizational-performance/our-insights/help-your-employees-find-purpose-or-watch-them-leave.
8 Lleó de Nalda, Á., A. Montaner, A. C. Edmondson, and P. Sotok. 2022. "Unlock the Power of Purpose." *MIT Sloan Management Review* 63(4): 20–24.

Chapter 10

Your Impact Lives On

The coffee in her hands had gone cold. She barely noticed.

We sat in a quiet corner of the conference venue, the buzz of post-session chatter fading around us. Across from me sat two colleagues. One early in her leadership journey, the other a seasoned executive approaching retirement.

The younger woman shifted in her seat, fingers tightening around her cup. "I know what I want – a promotion, bigger projects. But sometimes I stop and think, does any of it actually matter in the long run? How do you even think about legacy when you're still trying to prove yourself?"

The older executive leaned back in his chair, a knowing smile crossing his face. "That's the thing. Legacy isn't something you figure out at the end. You start shaping it from day one. Every choice you make, every person you help, every moment you show up, whether you realize it or not, you're already building it."

I listened, reflecting on my own journey.

For years, I had chased the next milestone. Delivering results, earning promotions, and making an impact in ways that looked good on paper. But the moments that truly stayed with me weren't the title changes or the big wins.

They were the people I mentored, the cultures I helped shape, and the unexpected messages from colleagues who told me, *You changed how I see my career. You made me believe in myself.*

Legacy isn't something you plan for *someday*. It's crafted in the everyday decisions, the way you show up when no one is watching, and the impact you create in moments that don't make the headlines.

Early in our careers, success is defined by achievement – climbing ladders, proving ourselves, and striving for excellence. David Brooks[1] calls this the first mountain, where the focus is on *what I can accomplish*. But for those who keep climbing, another summit appears on the second mountain, where meaning is found not in personal success but in contribution, service, and impact.

DOI: 10.4324/9781003627265-11

The right questions become:

Am I using my experience to lift others?

What will remain long after I've moved on?

What legacy am I leaving in the hearts and minds of those I've influenced?

True leadership isn't about reaching the summit alone. It's about ensuring others can climb their mountains, too.

As we continue this chapter, we will explore how leaders can embed their legacy into their work to build systems that outlast individual contributions, mentor the next generation, and cultivate environments where leadership becomes a shared and ongoing force. The greatest impact is not found in what a leader accomplishes alone but in what continues long after their final decision.

Why Legacy Matters

The black car rolled forward, swallowed by the restless rhythm of Manhattan's streets. Beside me sat one of my company's CEOs, flipping through notes and refining our talking points for the event ahead.

We were on our way to the United Nations building, about to take part in the official launch of *Together for Safer Roads*. This ambitious initiative was, at the time, little more than an audacious vision shared among a small group of leaders who believed that corporate power could be a force for good.

I sat back momentarily, letting my mind drift beyond the towering skyline. The weight of the moment settled over me, not just as a corporate representative but as someone who had been in the trenches in the early meetings when *none* of us quite knew how this was going to take shape. There had been no blueprint, no guarantees of success, only an unwavering belief that if we pooled our influence, resources, and expertise, we could shift the needle on one of the world's most preventable crises.

I remembered those first gatherings. Conference rooms filled with uncertainty and ambition in equal measure. The statistics were sobering. Road crashes were among the leading causes of death worldwide, and yet, they rarely commanded the urgency they deserved. We asked hard questions: *What could we do? How could we make a difference?* The answers weren't clear at first, but we knew that waiting for perfect clarity meant waiting too long.

And now, years later, here we were. Driving through the streets of New York City toward the UN, not just as participants, but as *founding members*. This was no longer just an idea. It was a movement.

Years have passed since that day. I no longer sit in those meetings and no longer have a seat at that particular table. But I watch from the sidelines, and I see the ripples of what we created. *Together for Safer Roads* is thriving, evolving, and expanding its reach. The world moves fast, and corporate priorities shift, but this initiative, the one we helped launch, continues to save lives.

There's a lesson in that. The impact we make isn't always immediate. Often, it's the small ideas that we bravely share when we take a leap of faith and trust in a collective vision. Legacy isn't built-in grand announcements or headline moments. It's built on the quiet persistence of believing that change is possible, long before the world takes notice.

After all, legacy extends beyond individual accomplishments, shaping the people, systems, and cultures that carry a leader's influence forward. The true impact of leadership is not confined to a single moment but embedded in the values and structures that guide future generations.

Dr. Erik Erikson,[2] a renowned developmental psychologist, described this as generativity, or the deep desire to contribute to something larger than oneself, ensuring that progress continues long after direct involvement ends.

As leaders evolve, their focus shifts from personal success to lasting significance. Achievements matter, but the most meaningful contributions come from building something that empowers others to grow, adapt, and lead in their own right. Leadership is not about the name attached to an initiative but the foundation left behind.

Research[3] shows that individuals who engage in generative activities experience greater life satisfaction, a stronger sense of purpose, and enhanced well-being. In leadership, this translates into higher levels of engagement, fulfillment, and longevity. Leaders who focus on legacy are more likely to foster strong, values-driven organizations, where employees feel connected to a mission that outlasts any single person.

Legacy is the natural culmination of purpose-driven leadership. Throughout this book, we've explored how purpose fuels motivation, resilience, and innovation. But purpose alone is sometimes not enough. It must be sustained, reinforced, and ultimately passed on. As we continue this chapter, we will explore the tangible ways leaders can embed their legacy into their work, ensuring that their impact is not just felt today but extends well into the future.

Legacy: What Will You Leave Behind?

Legacy isn't something you decide to build one day. It's happening right now in the conversations you have, the decisions you make, and the people you invest in. Every moment, you're shaping the story people will tell about your leadership when you're not in the room.

I used to think legacy was about the big things. The grand initiatives, the policies with my name attached, and the programs I helped create. But looking back, I see it differently. Legacy isn't about what you do. It's about what endures when you're gone.

Values That Last

At the heart of every lasting legacy is a leader's values. Not the ones printed on a company website, but the ones you actually live by when no one is watching. Integrity, courage, and authenticity aren't just buzzwords. They're the markers of leadership that stick.

As a former executive at big companies, I had the privilege of sitting in rooms where we weren't just discussing business. We were working on ideas that would change the world.

But here's the thing about legacy: you don't always know, in the moment, how big something will become. You show up, you put in the work, and years later, you step back and see that the seeds you planted have grown into something far beyond you.

I'm no longer in those rooms, but I don't need to be. The work carries on. That's legacy.

Multiplying Impact through Others

One of the biggest mistakes leaders make? Thinking legacy is about them.

It's not.

Dr. K. Anders Ericsson's research[4] on expertise and mentorship reinforces what we instinctively know. Legacy isn't built alone. It's passed on. The best leaders don't just build careers. They create movements, investing in people who will go on to shape the future in ways they never imagined.

I've mentored people who have gone on to lead organizations, transform industries, and create policies I could never have envisioned. Watching them thrive has meant more than any title I've ever held.

If your success dies the moment you walk out the door, was it ever really success?

Systems That Sustain Impact

Beyond people, the strongest legacies are embedded in systems that sustain impact long after leadership changes. Peter Senge's work[5] on learning organizations highlights the power of systems thinking, creating interconnected structures that don't rely on one person but function effectively over time. After all, the best leaders don't just create change. They design mechanisms that keep it alive. It might look like policies that prioritize safety, inclusion, and innovation; leadership programs that develop future changemakers; or cultures that reward long-term thinking over short-term wins.

Organizations that crumble when a leader leaves were never strong to begin with. Those that thrive? They've built legacy into their operating models, ensuring the mission carries forward, regardless of who's in charge.

The Shift from Short-Term Wins to Long-Term Significance

So many leaders get caught up chasing short-term wins, focusing on the quarterly results, the promotions, and the high-profile projects. I've been there. I've felt the adrenaline of a big announcement and the satisfaction of delivering on a tough deadline.

But real leadership is about the long game. The leaders who make the biggest impact aren't obsessed with what they can achieve right now. They're thinking about what will still matter 10, 20, or 50 years from now.

If you want to build a legacy that lasts, ask yourself:

What will people say about my leadership when I'm no longer here?

How will my influence continue to shape the people and organizations I've worked with?

Have I created something that will outlast me?

Journaling, mentorship debriefs, and honest self-reflection keep leaders focused on what matters. After all, legacy-minded leaders are those who intentionally shape the future.

Legacy Evolves

The world changes. Industries shift. What worked yesterday won't always work tomorrow. The best leaders don't cling to what was. They evolve with what's next.

That means checking in regularly:

Are the people I've mentored thriving and passing on what they've learned?

Do the systems I built still support growth and innovation?

Does my influence still hold weight in the conversations that matter?

Legacy is about letting go and trusting that what you've built will stand without you. That's the test of leadership.

The Real Measure of Legacy

No one's legacy is defined by job titles or end-of-year reports. The measure of a leader's impact lives in the people they empower, the cultures they shape, and the change that continues long after they've moved on.

Policies fade. Power shifts. However, the leaders who truly change the game leave behind resilient organizations, inspired individuals, and a vision that carries forward to shape the next generation.

So the real question isn't just *What legacy am I leaving?* but *How am I ensuring it stands the test of time?*

Crafting Your Leadership Legacy: Actionable Steps

Legacy is the result of intentional leadership choices made over time. Every decision, interaction, and initiative contributes to the story of your leadership. The most impactful legacies are built with foresight, authenticity, and a commitment to developing others.

The foundation of your legacy lies in understanding your core values and purpose, which we discussed in Chapter 3. Taking the time to reflect on the principles that have guided your leadership journey allows you to clarify what truly matters. These values shape your decisions, the culture you foster, and the impact you leave behind.

Mentorship is a powerful way to extend your influence. Identifying high-potential individuals and investing time in their growth creates a ripple effect of leadership excellence. By sharing knowledge, modeling ethical leadership, and offering guidance, you empower the next generation to build upon your contributions.

Legacy extends beyond individuals. It is also embedded in the structures and systems you create. Designing self-sustaining governance frameworks and decision-making processes ensures organizational success beyond your direct involvement. When leaders build resilient structures, they make an enduring framework that supports future innovation and stability.

Encouraging a culture where experimentation, curiosity, and forward-thinking are valued ensures that the organization remains dynamic and adaptable. A future-oriented organization embraces challenges, explores new possibilities, and continuously evolves. This commitment to innovation strengthens an organization's long-term sustainability.

People remember how you made them feel, how you treated them, and how consistently your actions aligned with your values. Authenticity builds trust, and trust is the cornerstone of any enduring legacy. Leading with integrity fosters deep connections, strengthens workplace culture, and ensures your leadership impact is positive and lasting.

As you reach the end of this book, take a moment to look ahead. Imagine the influence you want to have, the lives you want to touch, and the enduring impact you aim to create. This is your opportunity to lead with purpose, resilience, and innovation to craft a legacy that reflects your deepest values while uplifting those around you.

Every choice you make, every relationship you build, and every challenge you navigate with courage contributes to your leadership story. The journey isn't about perfection. It's about intentionality. It's about showing up purposefully, embracing growth, and creating a foundation for others to thrive.

As you move forward, consider this your call to action:

- Lead with purpose. Let your values shape your decisions, actions, and interactions.
- Cultivate resilience. Embrace challenges, adapt to change, and foster a culture of strength.
- Inspire innovation. Encourage forward-thinking, calculated risk-taking, and visionary leadership.
- Invest in others. Mentor, uplift, and empower those around you, knowing your legacy continues through their growth and success.

Your legacy begins now. Lead with integrity, invest in others, and create a leadership legacy that truly matters. The future is waiting, and your impact will shape it in ways that transcend time.

Notes

1 Brooks, D. 2020. *The Second Mountain: The Quest for a Moral Life*. Random House.
2 Erikson, E. H. 1950. *Childhood and Society*. W.W. Norton & Company.
3 Ryff, C. D. 2014. "Psychological Well-being Revisited: Advances in the Science and Practice of Eudaimonia." *Psychotherapy and Psychosomatics* 83(1): 10–28. https://doi.org/10.1159/000353263.
4 Ericsson, K. A., and R. Pool. 2017. *Peak: Secrets from the New Science of Expertise*. Houghton Mifflin Harcourt.
5 Senge, P. M. 2006. *The Fifth Discipline: The Art and Practice of the Learning Organization* (2nd ed.). Doubleday.

Chapter 11

30-Day Challenge

Day 1: Career Check-In

"Where are you right now?" Reflect on your current role. What's working well? What isn't? Identify one thing you're proud of and one area needing improvement.

Task: Write a brief career summary and highlight one immediate action to improve your current situation.

Day 2: Define Your Daily Non-Negotiables

Identify the key activities that drive your success each day. These are your "non-negotiables."

Task: List three to five daily non-negotiables that you must achieve to feel successful.

Day 3: Declutter Your Mind

Mental clutter can hold you back. Learn techniques to clear your mind and focus on what matters.

Task: Spend ten minutes doing a brain dump – write down everything on your mind. Then prioritize the top three things to focus on.

Day 4: Micro-Meditations

Introduce the power of micro-meditations – short, intentional pauses during your day.

Task: Practice three micro-meditations today. Each should last one to three minutes. Reflect on how it impacts your focus and stress levels.

Day 5: Skill Sharpening

Focus on improving one key skill that aligns with your career goals.

DOI: 10.4324/9781003627265-12

Task: Spend 30 minutes today working on that skill, whether it's reading an article, watching a tutorial, or practicing.

Day 6: Daily Success Ritual

Establish a daily ritual that sets you up for success, such as a morning routine or end-of-day reflection.

Task: Create and implement your ritual today.

Day 7: Weekly Wins and Reflections

Reflect on the past week. What were your biggest wins? What challenges did you overcome?

Task: Write a reflection on your week.

Day 8: Set a Micro-Goal

Set a small, specific goal that you can achieve today. Micro-goals build momentum.

Task: Achieve your micro-goal today.

Day 9: Networking Outreach

Networking is key to career growth. Today, focus on connecting with someone new in your field.

Task: Reach out to one new contact, whether it's through LinkedIn or a quick email.

Day 10: Professional Development Plan

Create a simple plan for ongoing professional development.

Task: Identify one area for growth and find a course, book, or resource to develop that skill.

Day 11: Social Media Audit

Your online presence matters. Today, audit your LinkedIn profile or other professional social media.

Task: Update your profile with recent achievements, new skills, or a fresh headline.

Day 12: Learn from a Mentor

Mentorship can accelerate your growth. Identify a mentor or someone you admire.

Task: Reach out to a mentor for advice or schedule a conversation.

Day 13: Elevator Pitch Refinement

Your elevator pitch is crucial for networking. Today, refine it.

Task: Write a concise, compelling elevator pitch that reflects your current career goals. Record yourself delivering it.

Day 14: Weekly Reflection

Reflect on the week's activities: what worked, what didn't?

Task: Write a short reflection on your week.

Day 15: Small Wins Day

Focus on achieving a series of small wins throughout the day to build momentum.

Task: Complete three small, actionable tasks that contribute to your career goals.

Day 16: Peer Feedback

Seek feedback from your peers to improve your work.

Task: Share a piece of work, idea, or project with a peer or the group and ask for constructive feedback. Reflect on how you can implement this feedback.

Day 17: Mid-Challenge Check-In

We're halfway through! It's time to check in on your progress.

Task: Review the goals you set at the beginning. Are you on track? Adjust your plan if needed.

Day 18: Productivity Boosters

Learn new techniques to enhance your productivity.

Task: Implement one productivity technique today, such as the Pomodoro Technique or time blocking. Reflect on how it impacted your day.

Day 19: Stress Management

Managing stress is vital for sustained performance. Explore quick stress-relief techniques.

Task: Practice a stress-management technique today, such as deep breathing or a quick walk.

Day 20: Project Push

Focus on advancing a specific project or task that's been lingering.

Task: Dedicate time to pushing forward a project that's been stuck.

Day 21: Weekly Review

Reflect on your progress and prepare for the final week.

Task: Write a weekly review focusing on your biggest achievements and areas to improve.

Day 22: Identify Your Zone of Genius

Your Zone of Genius is where your skills, passions, and impact align. It's what you do better than most and where you feel most fulfilled.

Task: Reflect on moments when you felt in flow, energized, and highly effective. Write down three to five activities or skills that represent your Zone of Genius and brainstorm one way to incorporate them more into your career.

Day 23: Update Your Resume

Refresh your resume with recent achievements and skills.

Task: Spend time updating your resume. Focus on highlighting the skills and achievements most relevant to your career goals.

Day 24: Personal Branding

Strengthen your personal brand by clarifying your unique value proposition.

Task: Write a personal branding statement that reflects your strengths and goals.

Day 25: Planning Your Next Steps

It's time to look ahead and plan your next steps beyond this challenge.

Task: Write down three actionable steps you'll take after the challenge ends.

Day 26: Professional Networking

Focus on expanding your professional network.

Task: Connect with three new professionals in your field. This could be through LinkedIn, at an event, or via mutual connections.

Day 27: Gratitude and Reflection

Practicing gratitude can enhance your outlook and motivation.

Task: Write a gratitude list focusing on what you've learned and achieved during the challenge.

Day 28: Final Push

Use today to complete any unfinished tasks or goals from the challenge.

Task: Choose one outstanding task or goal and complete it today.

Day 29: Career Blueprint Creation

It's time to put everything together and create a career blueprint.

Task: Compile your reflections, goals, and action plans into a single document – a career blueprint.

Day 30: Challenge Recap and Celebration

Congratulations! You've completed the 30-Day Career Activation Challenge. Let's celebrate your progress and look at what's next.

Task: Write a reflection on the entire challenge. What were your biggest takeaways? What will you do next?

Afterword

This book was born during a period of profound change in my life. A time of letting go, redefining, and learning to lead in new ways. It was not a straight path, nor an easy one. It was a path lined with doubt, heartbreak, and whispers of uncertainty. And yet, it was my path. And for that, I am grateful.

In June 2024, my career took an unexpected turn as my time in the corporate world ended. Or perhaps it was not surprising at all. Deep down, I had known for some time that this chapter of my life was closing – that the corporate world, the titles, and the battles fought in fluorescent-lit rooms had never indeed been mine to hold forever.

I spent decades in a world that asked me to be more, give more, and prove more. And yet, I felt the weight of misalignment pressing in. *Was this all there was?* The quiet gnawing at the edges of my soul suggested otherwise.

Leaving was not just about a job. It was about stepping into leadership differently. It was about reclaiming clarity, defining success on my terms, and recognizing that authentic leadership isn't about a title, but it's about impact. And yet, even as I built something new, the voices of doubt lingered. *Was I enough? Could I start over? Could I lead in a way that aligned with my values rather than corporate expectations?*

Then came the loss of a dear friend. Glenn was 53. His passing was a stark reminder of how fleeting our time is.

It forced me to reflect.

Not just about what I had done with my life but also about what I still had left to do. Leadership, I realized, isn't about chasing goals in a race against time. It's about presence. It's about the people we touch and the legacies we leave, not in spreadsheets but in lives.

Loss has a way of shaking us awake. Just as I was beginning to regain my footing, life dealt another blow. I got sick.

Eight days in the hospital. Eight days of uncertainty, fear, and surrendering to the reality that my body had limits I could no longer ignore. It wasn't

DOI: 10.4324/9781003627265-13

just the physical toll; it was the stark realization that, for all my years of striving to protect and care for others, I had neglected my own well-being. There was an irony to it. I had spent decades ensuring the health and safety of others, yet here I was, vulnerable and unprotected.

Lying there, I was forced to confront a truth I had long resisted.

Leadership shouldn't be about pushing harder, sacrificing more, or proving worth through exhaustion. It is about sustainability. It is about having the strength – physically, mentally, and emotionally – to lead with clarity, purpose, and vision. If I wanted to make an impact, I first had to care for myself. If I wanted to build something lasting, I needed to create from a place of strength, not depletion.

That experience reshaped how I think about leadership. It's not about achieving for the sake of achieving. It's about alignment. It's about knowing when to pause, when to listen, and when to let go. It's about making space, not just for yourself, but for what's possible.

The past year has been a journey of redefinition. Learning to trust that leadership isn't just about driving results but about shaping a legacy of impact. That clarity comes not from holding on but from making space for what truly matters. Letting go is not failure; it is the ultimate act of strength.

And every single day, I choose to make that space. I am shedding the layers that no longer serve me. I am stepping into the unknown, not with fear but with quiet confidence. I am choosing to lead differently. To build something that reflects not just where I have been but where I am going.

And if you are reading this, I know you, too, have stood at the edge of something uncertain. I see the weight of doubt, the ache of loss, the longing for something more. And I want you to know this: you are not alone. The call to something greater is not an illusion. It is not a mistake. It is real. And it is yours to follow.

So step forward. Make space for what is possible. Trust that your actions and intentions will shape the path ahead. Do the work, and then, when the time is right, let things unfold. Because what is meant for you, will find you.

And on the days when you falter, when the dream feels distant, you wonder if you have what it takes. Remember this: tomorrow is another chance to believe again.

Index

Note: *Italic* page numbers refer to figures.

For Product Safety Concerns and Information please contact our
EU representative GPSR@taylorandfrancis.com Taylor & Francis
Verlag GmbH, Kaufingerstraße 24, 80331 München, Germany